TALK TO ME IN KOREAN
LEVEL 1

From Greetings to Numbers,
Learn the Fundamentals of Conversational Korean

This book is based on a series of published lessons,
divided into ten levels, which are currently available
at https://talktomeinkorean.com.

Talk To Me In Korean - Level 1

1판 1쇄 · 1st edition published	2015. 9. 21.
1판 26쇄 · 26th edition published	2024. 5. 13.

지은이 · Written by	Talk To Me In Korean
책임편집 · Edited by	선경화 Kyung-hwa Sun, 스테파니 베이츠 Stephanie Bates
디자인 · Designed by	선윤아 Yoona Sun
삽화 · Illustrations by	김경해 Kyounghae Kim
녹음 · Voice Recordings by	선현우 Hyunwoo Sun, 최경은 Kyeongeun Choi
펴낸곳 · Published by	롱테일북스 Longtail Books
펴낸이 · Publisher	이수영 Su Young Lee
편집 · Copy-edited by	김보경 Florence Kim
주소 · Address	04033 서울특별시 마포구 양화로 113, 3층(서교동, 순흥빌딩)
	3rd Floor, 113 Yanghwa-ro, Mapo-gu, Seoul, KOREA
이메일 · E-mail	TTMIK@longtailbooks.co.kr
ISBN	979-11-86701-07-2 14710

*이 교재의 내용을 사전 허가 없이 전재하거나 복제할 경우 법적인 제재를 받게 됨을 알려 드립니다.

*잘못된 책은 구입하신 서점이나 본사에서 교환해 드립니다.

*정가는 표지에 표시되어 있습니다.

TTMIK - TALK TO ME IN KOREAN

MESSAGE
FROM
THE AUTHOR

Hi, everyone. My name is Hyunwoo Sun, and I am a co-founder and teacher at https://talktomeinkorean.com. The website was created in 2009 in order to help people learn Korean through simple and easily accessible lessons, and ever since then, we have experienced some amazing things! Talk To Me In Korean audio lessons have been downloaded over 100 million times, we have received messages and letters from people around the world telling us how fast their Korean is improving, and we have even met people who have approached us on the streets of Seoul and talked to us in Korean!

We are very happy to see our lessons published as books, and just like our online lessons, this book is designed to help you learn Korean on your own even if you do not have a teacher or do not have the opportunity to attend classroom lessons. When you study with this book, please make sure you practice saying everything you learn out loud so that your pronunciation will become more accurate, and you will gain more confidence when speaking the Korean language.

Learning to speak a new language is a life-changing experience, and we are very happy to be part of your journey toward that goal. If you have any questions about any part of the book while studying on your own, please feel free to ask us by e-mailing us, leaving a comment on our website, or sending us a message on social media. We are always here to support your efforts to learn Korean, and our ultimate goal is to see you "talk to us in Korean". Thank you very much. 감사합니다!

TABLE OF CONTENTS

8   *LESSON 1.* Hello, Thank you / 안녕하세요, 감사합니다

13 *LESSON 2.* Yes, No, What? / 네, 아니요

20 *LESSON 3.* Goodbye, See you / 안녕히 계세요, 안녕히 가세요

24 *LESSON 4.* I am sorry, Excuse me / 죄송합니다, 저기요

29 *LESSON 5.* It is me, What is it? / -이에요, -예요

34 *LESSON 6.* This is …, What is this? / 이거 …, 이거 뭐예요?

39 *LESSON 7.* This, That, It / 이, 저, 그, 거/것

45 *LESSON 8.* It is NOT me / 아니에요

50 *LESSON 9.* Topic/Subject Marking Particles / -은/는, -이/가

60 *LESSON 10.* Have, Do not have, There is, There is not / 있어요, 없어요

67 *[Blog]* Places in Korea: Han River (한강)

69 *LESSON 11.* Please give me … / … 주세요

75 *LESSON 12.* It is delicious, It tastes awful, Thank you for the food
        / 맛있어요, 잘 먹겠습니다

LESSON 13. I want to ··· / -고 싶어요   80

LESSON 14. What do you want to do? / 뭐 -고 싶어요?   85

LESSON 15. Sino-Korean Numbers / 일, 이, 삼, 사, ···   90

LESSON 16. Basic Present Tense / -아/어/여요   95

LESSON 17. Past Tense / -았/었/였어요   101

LESSON 18. Location Marking Particles / 어디, -에, -에서   107

LESSON 19. When / 언제   115

LESSON 20. Native Korean Numbers / 하나, 둘, 셋, 넷, ···   120

[Blog] Travel in Korea: Taking a Taxi   129

LESSON 21. Negative Sentences / 안, -지 않다   132

LESSON 22. Verbs / 하다   137

LESSON 23. Who? / 누구?   142

LESSON 24. Why? How? / 왜? 어떻게?   147

LESSON 25. From A To B, From C Until D / -에서/부터 -까지   152

[Answers]   158

LESSON 1

Hello, Thank you

안녕하세요. 감사합니다.

Track 01

안녕하세요.

Hello./Hi./How are you?/Good afternoon./Good evening./etc...

At first, it might be difficult to pronounce this greeting naturally, but after some practice, it will get easier.

안녕 + 하세요 = 안녕하세요.
[an-nyeong] [ha-se-yo] [an-nyeong-ha-se-yo.]

안녕 = well-being, peace, health

하세요 = you do, do you?, please do

안녕하세요 is the most common way of greeting someone in Korean. This greeting is in 존댓말, or polite/formal language. When someone greets you with 안녕하세요, you can
[jon-daen-mal]
simply greet the person back with 안녕하세요.

8

When you write this greeting, you can write it as "안녕하세요." (statement) or "안녕하세요?" (question form). Either way is perfectly acceptable. 안녕하세요 was originally a question asking "Are you doing well?", "Are you at peace?", or "Are you living well?", but since it is a very common expression, people began to not expect any special answers in reply. For example, when you ask a friend of yours "What's up?", do you really expect an honest answer about what is going on? In this case, you might hear "What's up?" in reply. 안녕하세요 is exactly like that.

Sample Conversation

A: 안녕하세요. = Hello.
B: 안녕하세요. = Hi.

Track 01

In Korean, there are a few levels of politeness which are commonly called "honorifics" in English. If you are a beginner learner, it might seem intimidating at first to learn of the honorifics, but it is important to know and utilize them. It gets much easier as you learn and practice more, so don't worry!

You can divide Korean honorifics into two categories that are quite easy to distinguish from each other and learn to use. One category is called 존댓말, which means polite or formal language, and the other is 반말, which means casual, intimate, or informal language.
[jon-daen-mal]
[ban-mal]
In Korean, if you hear sentences that end in '-요' or '-니다', they are most likely in 존댓말
[-yo]   [-ni-da]
(polite/formal language). It is better to learn 존댓말 first because if you speak 존댓말 in a situation when you can use 반말 (intimate/informal language), you are not going to be in too much trouble. However, if you use 반말 when you are supposed to use 존댓말, you might get into trouble.

감사합니다.
Thank you.

감사 + 합니다 = 감사합니다.
[gam-sa]   [ham-ni-da]   [gam-sa-ham-ni-da]

감사 = appreciation, thankfulness, gratitude

합니다 = I do, I am doing

Track 01

감사합니다 is the most common way to politely say "thank you". 감사 means "gratitude", and 합니다 means "I do" or "I am doing" in 존댓말 (polite/formal language). Together, the two mean "thank you". You can use 감사합니다 whenever you find yourself in a situation where you want to say "thank you".

In English, when you say "thank you", the expression has the word "you" in it. In Korean, however, people just say 감사합니다, but the word does not have an object ("you") in it. You do not have to say "you" in Korean because it is easy to guess to whom you are offering thanks. As you learn more Korean expressions, you will see that there are many that need not include the object within the sentence.

If you have a Korean friend or live in Korea but have not tried using these expressions, try to use them as often as possible until they become very easy and comfortable to say!

Sample Dialogue

Track 02

A: 안녕하세요.
　　[an-nyeong-ha-se-yo.]

B: 안녕하세요.
　　[an-nyeong-ha-se-yo.]

A: 여기요.
　　[yeo-gi-yo.]

B: 감사합니다.
　　[gam-sa-ham-ni-da.]

A: *Hello.*

B: *Hello.*

A: *Here you go.*

B: *Thank you.*

✏️ Exercises for Lesson 1

1. What is the most common Korean greeting when you want to say "hello", "good morning", "good afternoon", or "hi" to someone?

( )

2. How do you say "thank you" in polite/formal Korean?

( )

3. What is the term for referring to the polite/formal language in Korean?

a. [jan-so-ri]   b. [jon-daen-mal]   c. [han-gu-geo]   d. [an-nyeong]

4. Which term is used when referring to the intimate/informal language in Korean?

a. [jeong-mal]   b. [chu-ka-hae-yo]   c. [ban-mal]   d. [in-sa-mal]

5. When you hear a Korean sentence that ends in '-요' or '-니다', is the politeness level typically
[-yo]   [-ni-da]
존댓말 or 반말?

( )

LESSON 2

Yes, No, What?

> # 네. 아니요.

After studying with this lesson, you will be able to answer with either YES or NO in response to basic questions in Korean.

Track 03

네/아니요

In Korean, "Yes" is 네 and "No" is 아니요 in 존댓말, or polite/formal language.
[ne]   [a-ni-yo]   [jon-daen-mal]

네. = Yes.
[ne.]
아니요. = No.
[a-ni-yo.]

However, in Korean, when people say "네", it does not have the same meaning as saying "Yes" in English. The same goes for "아니요", too. This is because the Korean word "네" expresses your "agreement" to what the other person is saying. In contrast, "아니요" expresses your "disagreement" or "denial" to what the other person is saying.

13

For example, if someone asks you "You don't like coffee?" (커피 안 좋아해요?) in Korean and your answer is "No, I do not like coffee", you have to say "네". The literal translation of "네" is "Yes", but what you actually mean in English would be "No, I do not like coffee".

Strange? Maybe a little, so it is more accurate to put it this way:

네. = That is right. / I agree. / Sounds good. / What you said is correct.

아니요. = That is not right. / I do not agree. / What you said is not correct.

When you ask "You don't like coffee?" in Korean, if the person answering does not like coffee, he/she will say "No" in English but "네" in Korean. However, if the person DOES like coffee, he/she will say "Yes" in English but "아니요" in Korean.

Track 03

Sample Conversations

A: 커피 좋아해요? = Do you like coffee?
[keo-pi jo-a-hae-yo?]
B: 네. 좋아해요. = Yes, I like coffee.
[ne. jo-a-hae-yo.]

A: 커피 좋아해요? = Do you like coffee?
[keo-pi jo-a-hae-yo?]
B: 아니요. 안 좋아해요. = No, I do not like coffee.
[a-ni-yo. an jo-a-hae-yo.]

A: 커피 안 좋아해요? = You don't like coffee?
[keo-pi an jo-a-hae-yo?]
B: 아니요. 좋아해요. = Yes (아니요 in Korean), I like coffee.
[a-ni-yo. jo-a-hae-yo.]

A: 커피 안 좋아해요? = You don't like coffee?
[keo-pi an jo-a-hae-yo?]
B: 네. 안 좋아해요. = No (네 in Korean), I do not like coffee.
[ne. an jo-a-hae-yo.]

You do not have to worry about the other parts of the sample sentences mentioned previously. Just remember that the Korean system for saying YES and NO is different from the English system.

More usages of 네

네 is more than just YES or THAT IS RIGHT.
[ne]

While 네 is used to express "Yes" or "That is right", it is also used as a conversation filler. If you listen to two Korean people talking with each other, you will hear them saying 네 quite often, even when it is not intended to mean "Yes".

Therefore, it is normal for two Korean people to have a conversation as the one below. Imagine that the entire conversation is in Korean.

Track 03

Sample Conversation

A: You know what, I bought this book yesterday.

B: 네. (Oh, you did?)
[ne.]

A: And I really like it.

B: 네... (I see...)

A: But it is a bit too expensive.

B: 네. (I see!)

A: Do you know how much it was?

B: How much was it?

A: It was 3,000 dollars!

15

B: 네? (What?)
[ne?]

A: So I paid with my credit card.

B: 네... (I got it.)

A: But I still like it a lot because it is a book by Kyeong-eun Choi.

B: 네... (I see...)

Of course, that was just an example dialogue, and our books do not cost 3,000 dollars. So, as you can see from the dialogue above, 네 is a multi-player. Not only can it mean "yes" or
[ne]
"that is right", but it can also mean "I see", "I got it", "I am here! (when someone calls you)", "I understand", "ah-ha", or any other affirmative statement.

Using 네 with 맞아요

Track 03

Because 네 and 아니요 are focused more on your agreement and disagreement rather than
[ne]   [a-ni-yo]
whether something is true or not, and ALSO because 네 can mean "I see" or "ah-ha" as well, Korean people often add the expression 맞아요 after 네.
[ma-ja-yo]   [ne]

네, 맞아요. = Yes, that is right.
[ne, ma-ja-yo.]

This is used in order to express more strongly and clearly that you are saying "You are right" rather than sounding like you are just passively listening while nodding.

네 is amazing. It can be many things, but it can also be "What did you say?"

Suppose someone said something to you, but you could not hear the person well or you were not paying much attention. Then you can say "네?" to mean "Pardon me?", "I am
[ne?]

sorry?", "What did you say?", or "I did not hear you well". You can also use "네?" to show your surprise.

Sample Conversation

A: I bought a present for you.

B: 네? (What? You did?)
[ne?]

A: I said I bought a present for you!

B: 네? (What?)

A: Forget it.

B: 네? (Pardon?)

Track 03

Sample Dialogue

🎙️ Track 04

A: 경화 씨, 커피 좋아해요?
[gyeong-hwa ssi, keo-pi jo-a-hae-yo?]

B: 네, 좋아해요.
[ne, jo-a-hae-yo.]

A: 블랙커피 좋아해요?
[beul-laek-keo-pi jo-a-hae-yo?]

B: 네, 맞아요.
[ne, ma-ja-yo.]

A: Do you like coffee, Kyung-hwa?

B: Yes, I do.

A: Do you like black coffee?

B: Yes, that's right.

✏ Exercises for Lesson *2*

1. How do you say "yes" in polite/formal Korean?

( )

2. How do you say "no" in polite/formal Korean?

( )

3. What is the difference between the Korean "yes" and "no" and the English "yes" and "no" ?

a. The Korean "yes" and "no" are stronger than the English "yes" and "no".

b. The Korean "yes" and "no" express your agreement or disagreement to what the other person said, rather than expressing whether the fact itself is true or not.

c. In Korean, "no" does not exist. There is only "yes".

Check the answers on **p.159**

4. How do you say "that is right" in polite/formal Korean?

( )

5. Which of the following is NOT correct?

a. 네. = Yes.

b. 네. = I see.

c. 네? = Pardon me?

d. 네? = What? (showing one's surprise)

e. 네. = Thanks.

19

LESSON 3

Goodbye, See you

안녕히 계세요. 안녕히 가세요.

Track 05

After studying with this lesson, you will be able to say goodbye in Korean.

Do you remember how to say "Hello" in Korean? It is 안녕하세요.
[an-nyeong-ha-se-yo]

If you remember 안녕하세요, that is fantastic! If you even remember that "안녕" in 안녕하세요 means "peace" and "well-being", that is even more fantastic!

안녕 = well-being, peace, health.
[an-nyeong]

In Korean, when you say "goodbye" in formal/polite Korean, 존댓말, there are two types of
[jon-daen-mal]
expressions, and both of these expressions have the word 안녕 in them.
[an-nyeong]

One is when you are the one who is leaving. The other is when you are the one who is staying and you are seeing the people or the person leaving.

20

If you are leaving and the other person is (or the other people are) staying, you can say:

안녕히 계세요.

If you are staying and the other person is (or the other people are) leaving, you can say:

안녕히 가세요.

* If two or more people meet and all of them are leaving and going in separate directions, they can all say **안녕히 가세요** *to each other since no one is staying.*

For now, don't worry about the literal meaning of the expressions and just learn them as they are. However, if you are really curious and if you were to translate these greetings literally, they would be translated like this:

Track 05

안녕히 계세요. = Stay in peace.
[an-nyeong-hi gye-se-yo.]
안녕히 가세요. = Go in peace.
[an-nyeong-hi ga-se-yo.]

Again, don't worry about the literal meaning of these greetings JUST YET!

* When Korean people say **안녕하세요**, **안녕히 계세요**, *or* **안녕히 가세요**, *they do not*
               [an-nyeong-ha-se-yo] [an-nyeong-hi gye-se-yo]   [an-nyeong-hi ga-se-yo]
always pronounce EVERY single letter clearly. So often at times, what you would hear clearly is just the ending part, "**세요**".
                [se-yo]

Sample Dialogue

A: 안녕하세요.
[an-nyeong-ha-se-yo.]

B: 안녕하세요. 저는 이제 가요.
[an-nyeong-ha-se-yo. jeo-neun i-je ga-yo.]

A: 안녕히 가세요.
[an-nyeong-hi ga-se-yo.]

B: 네. 안녕히 계세요.
[ne. an-nyeong-hi gye-se-yo.]

A: Hello.

B: Hello. I'm leaving now.

A: Goodbye.

B: Okay. Goodbye.

✏ Exercises for Lesson **3**

1. If you are leaving a place and the others are staying, how do you say "goodbye" in polite/formal Korean? The literal translation of this expression is "please stay in peace".

( )

2. If you are the one staying and the others are leaving, how do you say "goodbye" in polite/formal Korean? The literal translation of this expression is "please go in peace".

( )

3. If both you and the other person are leaving the place you are in now, and no one is staying, what do you say to the other person to say "goodbye" in polite/formal Korean?

( )

4. What does 안녕 mean?

( )

Check the answers on **p.159**

LESSON **4**

I am sorry, Excuse me

죄송합니다. 저기요.

Track 07

After studying with this lesson, you will be able to say "I am sorry" or "I apologize" in Korean. You will also be able to get someone's attention when you want to say something to them or order something in a restaurant.

죄송합니다.

Do you remember how to say "Thank you" in Korean? It is 감사합니다. If you also remember
[gam-sa-ham-ni-da]
that 감사합니다 is basically 감사 ("appreciation" or "thankfulness") plus 합니다 ("I do"), you

can assume that 죄송합니다 is also 죄송 plus 합니다.
[joe-song-ham-ni-da]

죄송 means "apology", "being sorry", or "feeling ashamed", and 합니다 means "I do".
[joe-song]   [ham-ni-da]
Therefore, 죄송합니다 means "I am sorry" or "I apologize".
[joe-song-ham-ni-da]

Q: Why is "합니다" not pronounced as [hap-ni-da] but instead as [ham-ni-da]?

A: In Korean, when you say something like "합", you do not pronounce the final letter independently, but rather as a part of the entire syllable. Therefore, instead of pronouncing 합 as "ha" plus "p", you press your lips together after 합 without aspirating the "p" sound, which is also known as a "bilabial stop" (try saying the English word "stop" with a puff of air at the end [aspirated], then say "stop" again with your lips pressed together and no puff of air). Since the syllable which follows 합 is 니, there is no vowel in between ㅂ and ㄴ in order to create the aspirated "p" sound. This creates an easier transition between 합 and 니, and when spoken quickly, ㅂ softens to an ㅁ [m] sound.

"I am sorry" is NOT always 죄송합니다.

Track 07

Even though 죄송합니다 is BASICALLY "I am sorry", you cannot use 죄송합니다 when you
[joe-song-ham-ni-da]
want to say "I am sorry to hear that". Often at times, native Korean speakers are confused when delivering bad news to English-speaking friends and hear the phrase "I am sorry" as a response. If you say "I am sorry" after you hear some bad news from your Korean friend, he or she might say "Why are YOU apologizing for that?" to you. This is because 죄송합니다 ONLY means "I apologize", "It was my bad", "Excuse me" or "I should not have done that". It can never mean "I am sorry to hear that".

Using 죄송합니다 as "excuse me" in Korean is typically heard when passing through a crowd of people or when bumping into someone. It is NOT used the same way as the English phrase "excuse me", especially when it comes to trying to get the attention of a waiter or a stranger. When you want to get someone's attention in Korean, you absolutely need to use 저기요.
[jeo-gi-yo]

저기요.

저기 literally means "over there", so "저기요" means "Hey, you! Over there! Look at me!"
[jeo-gi]
but in a more polite way. You can say "저기요" when someone is not looking at you but you
need their attention. It is exactly the same as "Excuse me" except "저기요" does not mean "I
am sorry".

In English, you can use the expression "Excuse me" in all of the following situations:

1) when passing through a crowd of people;

2) when leaving the room for a second;

3) when you want to get someone's attention and talk to them or let them know something;

4) when you want to call the waiter in a restaurant or a cafe to order something.

Track 07

저기요 is an expression which CAN be translated as "excuse me", but only in numbers 3 and
[jeo-gi-yo]
4 listed above.

Including 죄송합니다, there are a few more expressions you can use when passing through a
crowd of people:

1. 잠시만요. (literal meaning: "Just a second")
   [jam-si-man-nyo.]
2. 죄송합니다. (literal meaning: "I am sorry")
   [joe-song-ham-ni-da.]
3. 잠깐만요. (literal meaning: "Just a second")
   [jam-kkan-man-nyo.]
(Yes, "잠시만요" and "잠깐만요" are the same thing.)

These are the most commonly used expressions. You do not have to memorize them right
now, but they are good to know!

26

Sample Dialogue

Track 08

A: 아야!
[a-ya!]

B: 죄송합니다.
[joe-song-ham-ni-da.]

A: 저기요! 이거요.
[jeo-gi-yo! i-geo-yo.]

A: Ouch!

B: I'm sorry.

A: Excuse me! Here it is.

27

✏ *Exercises for Lesson* **4**

1. If you made a mistake or did something that you feel bad about, what can you say in polite Korean to apologize?

(   )

2. You are running up the stairs inside a busy subway station and accidentally stepped on someone's foot. What can you say to the person to apologize?

(   )

3. You are in a restaurant and you are now ready to order. What do you say to the waiter to get his or her attention?

(   )

4. You want to pass through a crowd of people or reach out for a book in a bookstore, but there is someone in your way. Which of the following should you avoid saying to mean "excuse me"?

    a. 죄송합니다.
       [joe-song-ham-ni-da.]
    b. 잠시만요.
       [jam-si-man-nyo.]
    c. 안녕히 가세요.
       [an-nyeong-hi ga-se-yo.]

5. Which situation is most appropriate for saying "죄송합니다"?

    a. After you hear some bad news from a friend.

    b. When you are leaving the room for a second.

    c. When you want to get a person's attention and talk to them or let them know something.

    d. When you apologize to someone.

LESSON 5

It is me, What is it?

-이에요/-예요

After studying with this lesson, you will be able to say things like "A is B (noun)" or "I am ABC (noun)" in polite/formal Korean.

Track 09

-이에요/-예요

-이에요 and -예요 have a similar role to that of the English verb "to be". The fundamental
[-i-e-yo]   [-ye-yo]

difference, however, is the sentence structure and order that they are used in.

English sentence structure: [be] + ABC.   * *ABC is a noun here.*

   Ex) It is ABC. / I am ABC.

Korean sentence structure: ABC + [be].   * *ABC is a noun here.*

   Ex) ABC예요. = It is ABC. / I am ABC.
   [ABC-ye-yo.]

29

In English, the verb "to be" is changed to "am", "are", or "is" depending on the subject of the sentence, but in Korean, you decide whether to use -이에요 or -예요 depending on whether
[-i-e-yo]   [-ye-yo]
the last letter of the previous word ends in a consonant or a vowel. -이에요 and -예요 are very similar and also sound similar, so it is not a big problem if you mix up these two, but it is still better to know the correct forms.

When you want to say that "It is ABC" in Korean, and if the word for "ABC" has a final consonant in the last letter, you add -이에요. However, if it does not have a final consonant
[-i-e-yo]
and ends in a vowel, you add -예요. This is just to make the pronunciation easier, so it will
[-ye-yo]
come naturally if you practice with some sample sentences.

Track 09

Conjugation

Final consonant + -이에요
[-i-e-yo]
No final consonant (Only vowel) + -예요
[-ye-yo]

Sample Sentences

물이에요. = 물 + -이에요
[mul + -i-e-yo]
(It is) water.

가방이에요. = 가방 + -이에요
[ga-bang + -i-e-yo]
(It is) a bag.

사무실이에요. = 사무실 + -이에요
[sa-mu-sil + -i-e-yo]
(It is) an office.

30

학교예요. = 학교 + -예요
[hak-kkyo + -ye-yo]
(It is) a school.

저예요. = 저 + -예요
[jeo + -ye-yo]
(It is) me.

As you can see from the examples above, in Korean, you do not have to use articles like "a/an" or "the" as in English. When you look up a noun in your Korean dictionary, you can add -이에요 or -예요 so that it will mean "It is ABC", "That is DEF", "I am XYZ".

You can also make this a question simply by raising the tone at the end of the sentence.

Sample Sentences

Track 09

물이에요. = It is water.
[mu-ri-e-yo.]
물이에요? = Is that water? Is this water?
[mu-ri-e-yo?]

학생이에요. = I am a student.
[hak-ssaeng-i-e-yo.]
학생이에요? = Are you a student?
[hak-ssaeng-i-e-yo?]

학교예요. = It is a school.
[hak-kkyo-ye-yo.]
학교예요? = Is it a school? Are you at school now?
[hak-kkyo-ye-yo?]

뭐 = What
[mwo]
뭐예요? = What is it? What is that?
[mwo-ye-yo?]

Sample Dialogue

Track 10

A: 뭐예요?
[mwo-ye-yo?]

B: 장난감이에요.
[jang-nan-kka-mi-e-yo.]

A: 장난감이에요?
[jang-nan-kka-mi-e-yo?]

A: What is it?

B: It's a toy.

A: Is it a toy?

✏ Exercises for Lesson **5**

The ending for the verb "to be," as in "this is an apple," in Korean is 이에요 *or* 예요. *Which one*
[i-e-yo]   [ye-yo]
of these endings you use depends on whether the last letter of the word that comes before it is a
consonant or a vowel. Choose which ending should be used after each noun.

1. 학생 + ( )
[hak-ssaeng]
student

2. 의자 + ( )
[ui-ja]
chair

3. 이거 + ( )
[i-geo]
this one

4. 집 + ( )
[jip]
house

5. 진짜 + ( )
[jin-jja]
real

Read the following English words or phrases, translate them to Korean, then say the words or phrases
aloud in Korean.

6. Water

( )

7. What

( )

8. What is it?

( )

9. It is me.

( )

10. School

( )

Check the answers on **p.159**

LESSON 6

This is ···, What is this?

> # 이거 ···, 이거 뭐예요?

Track 11

After studying with this lesson, you will be able to say "This is ABC" and also ask "Is this ABC?" and "What is this?" in polite/formal Korean.

In the previous lesson, you learned how -이에요 and -예요 can be placed after a noun to
express the meaning of "It is ABC" or "I am DEF".

Conjugation

Final consonant + -이에요
[-i-e-yo]
No final consonant (Only vowel) + -예요
[-ye-yo]

Sample Sentences

책 + -이에요 = 책이에요. = It is a book.
[chaek] [-i-e-yo] [chae-gi-e-yo]
저 + -예요 = 저예요. = It is me.
[jeo] [-ye-yo] [jeo-ye-yo]

* -이에요 *and* -예요 *have a similar role to that of the English verb* "to be".

34

How to say "THIS"

이거 = this, this one

이 ("this") + 것 ("thing") = 이것 → 이거
[i]　　　　　　[geot]　　　　　　[i-geot]　　[i-geo]

이거 can be found in the dictionary as 이것, which is originally how it was spelled and
[i-geo]　　　　　　　　　　　　　　　[i-geot]
pronounced, but over time, people began using 이거 for ease of pronunciation.
　　　　　　　　　　　　　　　　　　　　　[i-geo]

Sample Sentences

책이에요. = It is a book.
[chae-gi-e-yo.]
이거 책이에요. = This is a book.
[i-geo chae-gi-e-yo.]

Track 11

카메라예요. = It is a camera.
[ka-me-ra-ye-yo.]
이거 카메라예요. = This is a camera.
[i-geo ka-me-ra-ye-yo.]

커피예요. = It is coffee.
[keo-pi-ye-yo.]
이거 커피예요. = This is coffee.
[i-geo keo-pi-ye-yo.]

사전이에요. = It is a dictionary.
[sa-jeo-ni-e-yo.]
이거 사전이에요. = This is a dictionary.
[i-geo sa-jeo-ni-e-yo.]

이거 뭐예요? = What is this?

In Lesson 5, we introduced the question "뭐예요?" which means "What is it?" in Korean. You
　　　　　　　　　　　　　　　　　[mwo-ye-yo?]
can add "이거" in front of "뭐예요?" to ask "What is this?"
　　　　[i-geo]

35

Sample Conversations

A: 이거 뭐예요? = What is this?
[i-geo mwo-ye-yo?]
B: 이거 마이크예요. = This is a microphone.
[i-geo ma-i-keu-ye-yo.]

A: 이거 뭐예요? = What is this?
[i-geo mwo-ye-yo?]
B: 이거 핸드폰이에요. = This is a cellphone.
[i-geo haen-deu-po-ni-e-yo.]

A: 이거 뭐예요? = What is this?
[i-geo mwo-ye-yo?]
B: 이거 물이에요. = This is water.
[i-geo mu-ri-e-yo.]

A: 이거 뭐예요? = What is this?
[i-geo mwo-ye-yo?]
B: 이거 커피예요. = This is coffee.
[i-geo keo-pi-ye-yo.]

Track 11

Do you remember how to say "No"?

Sample Conversation

A: 이거 커피예요? = Is this coffee?
[i-geo keo-pi-ye-yo?]
B: 아니요. 이거 물이에요. = No. This is water.
[a-ni-yo. i-geo mu-ri-e-yo.]

Do you remember how to say "Yes, that is right"?

Sample Conversation

A: 이거 커피예요? = Is this coffee?
[i-geo keo-pi-ye-yo?]
B: 네. 맞아요. 이거 커피예요. = Yes, that is right. This is coffee.
[ne. ma-ja-yo. i-geo keo-pi-ye-yo]

Sample Dialogue

Track 12

A: 이거 볼펜이에요?
  [i-geo bol-pe-ni-e-yo?]

B: 아니요. 샤프예요.
  [a-ni-yo. sya-peu-ye-yo.]

A: 이거는요? 볼펜이에요?
  [i-geo-neun-nyo? bol-pe-ni-e-yo?]

B: 네, 볼펜 맞아요.
  [ne, bol-pen ma-ja-yo.]

A: Is this a ballpoint pen?

B: No. It is a mechanical pencil.

A: How about this? Is it a ballpoint pen?

B: Yes, that is a ballpoint pen.

Check the answers on **p.159**

1. How would you say "what is this?" in polite/formal Korean?

( )

2. Translate "this is a book" to Korean using polite/formal speech.

( )

Fill in the blanks with a Korean word to make the Korean and English sentences have the same meaning.

3. ( ) 커피예요?
= Is this coffee?

4. ( ) ( ) 커피예요.
= Yes, that is right. This is coffee.

5. ( ) 물이에요.
= No. It is water.

LESSON **7**

This, That, It

이, 저, 그, 거/것

Track **13**

In this lesson, you will learn how to say "this", "that", and "it" in Korean. In English, the words "this" and "that" can be used on their own (as pronouns) and to modify other words (as adjectives), but in Korean, the words for "this", "that", and "it" change their forms depending on whether they are pronouns or adjectives.

For example, you can say "this is my car" and "this car is mine" in English. The word "this" plays two different roles here: as a pronoun and as a word which modifies "car". In Korean, however, words for "this" as a modifier and "this" as "this item here" or "this thing here" are strictly distinguished, and the same is true for "that".

이 = this (near you)

이 커피 = this coffee
[i keo-pi]
이 컴퓨터 = this computer
[i keom-pyu-teo]
이 아이스크림 = this ice-cream
[i a-i-seu-keu-rim]

이 호텔 = this hotel
[i ho-tel]
이 택시 = this taxi
[i taek-si]
이 버스 = this bus
[i beo-seu]
이 카메라 = this camera
[i ka-me-ra]
이 피자 = this pizza
[i pi-ja]

저 = that (over there)

If you know how to say "I" in polite/formal Korean, it is the same thing. It sounds the same. However, you do not have to worry about being confused, because "저" is a modifier which modifies a different word, so it is always followed by a noun. The word for "I", "저", is followed by particles, verbs, etc. They are used in completely different contexts.

Track 13

저 마이크 = that microphone over there
[jeo ma-i-keu]
저 테이블 = that table over there
[jeo te-i-beul]
저 레스토랑 = that restaurant over there
[jeo re-seu-to-rang]

그 = the / that (near the other person)

"그" and "저" are both used for referring to something that is far away from the speaker.
[geu]   [jeo]
However, "그" is used when you are talking to the other person and the object is near that other person and far away from you. "저" is used for referring to something that is far away from both you and the other person.

Since 이, 그, and 저 can only work as modifiers in Korean, when you want to use "this", "that", or "it" as pronouns, either 거 or 것 need to follow 이, 그, or 저.
[geo]   [geot]

40

거 = 것 = thing, item, stuff, fact

Therefore:

이 = this
[i]

이 + 것 = 이것 or 이거 = this thing, this item, this one
      [i-geot]   [i-geo]

그 = the, that
[geu]

그 + 것 = 그것 or 그거 = the thing, the item, that one, it
      [geu-geot]   [geu-geo]

저 = that (over there)
[jeo]

저 + 것 = 저것 or 저거 = that thing over there
      [jeo-geot]   [jeo-geo]

You must not use either 거 or 것 when you point at a person.

Track
13

> Q: What if you do not see that thing, that object, or that person in your sight? What if it is not there? How do you refer to it?
>
> A: It is very simple. Just use the word "그" or "그것".

You can form various expressions using 이, 그, or 저 along with other words.

사람 = a person
[sa-ram]

이 사람 = this person, this man here, this lady here, he, she
[i sa-ram]

그 사람 = the person, that person, he, she
[geu sa-ram]

저 사람 = that person over there, he, she
[jeo sa-ram]

41

Sample Dialogue

A: 석진 씨, 이 브랜드 좋아해요?
[seok-jjin ssi, i beu-raen-deu jo-a-hae-yo?]

B: 아니요.
[a-ni-yo.]

A: 그럼 저 브랜드 좋아해요?
[geu-reom jeo beu-raen-deu jo-a-hae-yo?]

B: 네, 좋아해요.
[ne, jo-a-hae-yo.]

A: Seokjin, do you like this brand?

B: No.

A: Then do you like that brand over there?

B: Yes, I do.

✎ Exercises for Lesson 7

Match the Korean word to the English word of the same meaning.
There may be several Korean words for one English word.

1. 이거
   [i-geo]

2. 저것
   [jeo-geot]

3. 그거
   [geu-geo]

4. 그것
   [geu-geot]

5. 저거
   [jeo-geo]

6. 이것
   [i-geot]

a. this one
   (near you)

b. that one
   (far from you and near the other person)

c. that one over there
   (far from both you and the other person)

7. How do you say "what is that over there?" in polite/formal Korean?

(   )

8. How do you say "this computer" in Korean?

(   )

Fill in the blanks with a Korean word to make the Korean and English sentences have the same meaning.

9. 그거 (   ) 예요?

= What is it?

10. 저거 뭐 (   )? 저거 커피 (   )?

= What is that? Is that coffee over there?

Check the answers on **p.159**

44

LESSON 8

It is NOT me

아니에요.

In this lesson, you can learn how to say "not" or "something is NOT something".

아니에요 = to be not, it is not, you are not

아니에요 is the present tense form in the polite/formal language of the verb 아니다 (to be
[a-ni-e-yo]
not). So 아니에요 means "it is not", "I am not", "you are not", "he/she is not", etc.
[a-ni-e-yo]

* As you will notice later on, all Korean verbs end in "-다" in the dictionary. When you look up a

word and it ends in "-다", that is most likely a verb.

Whenever you want to say that something is NOT something, you can say the subject and

then add 아니에요.
[a-ni-e-yo]

Conjugation

Noun + 아니에요 = To be not + Noun

Sample Sentences

저 아니에요. = It is not me.

우유 아니에요. = It is not milk.

물 아니에요. = It is not water.

If you want to say "This is not milk", "I am not a student", "That is not a park", and so on, you can add the noun at the beginning of the sentence.

Sample Sentences

milk = 우유
[u-yu]
not milk = 우유 아니에요.
[u-yu a-ni-e-yo.]
This is not milk. = 이거 우유 아니에요.
[i-geo u-yu a-ni-e-yo.]

student = 학생
[hak-ssaeng]
not a student = 학생 아니에요.
[hak-ssaeng a-ni-e-yo.]
I am not a student. = 저 학생 아니에요.
[jeo hak-ssaeng a-ni-e-yo.]

hat = 모자
[mo-ja]
not a hat = 모자 아니에요.
[mo-ja a-ni-e-yo.]
That is not a hat. = 저거 모자 아니에요.
[jeo-geo mo-ja a-ni-e-yo.]

cat = 고양이
[go-yang-i]

not a cat = 고양이 아니에요.
[go-yang-i a-ni-e-yo.]

It is not a cat. = 그거 고양이 아니에요.
[geu-geo go-yang-i a-ni-e-yo.]

tiger = 호랑이
[ho-rang-i]

not a tiger = 호랑이 아니에요.
[ho-rang-i a-ni-e-yo.]

It is not a tiger. = 그거 호랑이 아니에요.
[geu-geo ho-rang-i a-ni-e-yo.]

Track 15

47

Sample Dialogue

Track
16

A: 석진 씨, 그거 쥐예요?
[seok-jjin ssi, geu-geo jwi-ye-yo?]

B: 아니요, 이거 쥐 아니에요.
[a-ni-yo, i-geo jwi a-ni-e-yo.]

A: 그럼 강아지예요?
[geu-reom gang-a-ji-ye-yo?]

B: 네, 맞아요.
[ne, ma-ja-yo.]

A: Seokjin, is that a rat?

B: No. This is not a rat.

A: Then is it a puppy?

B: Yes, that's right.

✎ Exercises for Lesson 8

1. In Korean, 우유 is "milk". How do you say "this is NOT milk"?
[u-yu]

(   )

2. In Korean, 모자 is "hat". How do you say "it is NOT a hat"?
[mo-ja]

(   )

3. In Korean, 사자 means "lion". How do you say "it is NOT a lion"?
[sa-ja]

(   )

4. If 저 means "I" in polite Korean, and 학생 is "student", how would you say "I am NOT a
[jeo]   [hak-ssaeng]
student"?

(   )

5. Since "my fault" in polite Korean is "제 잘못", write "it is not my fault" in Korean.
[je jal-mot]

(   )

Check the answers on **p.160**

LESSON 9

Topic/Subject Marking Particles

-은/는, -이/가

Track 17

You will learn about topic marking particles and subject marking particles in Korean with this lesson. Most languages do not have subject marking particles or topic marking particles in their sentences, so the concept might be very new to you. However, once you get used to them, knowing how to use these particles will come in handy.

If a noun which you want to talk about is the topic of the sentence, you use topic marking particles. If a word that you want to talk about is the subject of the verb of the sentence, you use subject marking particles. It sounds very simple, but when it comes to really using particles, it is a bit more complicated.

Topic marking particles : -은/는

The main role of topic marking particles is letting the listener know what you are talking about or going to talk about. Topic marking particles are placed after a noun to indicate THAT noun is the topic.

50

Conjugation

Word ending with a final consonant + -은
[-eun]

Word ending with a vowel + -는
[-neun]

Ex)

이 책 = this book
[i chaek]

이 책 + 은 = 이 책은
[i chaek]   [eun]   [i chae-geun]

가방 = bag
[ga-bang]

가방 + 은 = 가방은
[ga-bang]   [eun]   [ga-bang-eun]

이 차 = this car
[i cha]

이 차 + 는 = 이 차는
[i cha]   [neun]   [i cha-neun]

저 = I
[jeo]

저 + 는 = 저는
[jeo]   [neun]   [jeo-neun]

Track 17

If you just say "이 책", people will not know what it is about the book you are going to speak of; whether it is the subject of the sentence or the object of the sentence, no one will know. Topic marking particles and subject marking particles will help make your sentence clearer so that even if you do not finish your sentence, the listener will know what role the noun plays if you use the right particle.

The topic of the sentence, marked by -은 or -는, is usually (but not always) the same as the
[-eun]   [-neun]
subject of the sentence.

저 = I
[jeo]

저 + 는 = 저는 = as for me / I (who is talking)
[neun]   [jeo-neun]

저는 학생이에요. = As for me, I am a student. / I am a student.
[jeo-neun hak-ssaeng-i-e-yo.]

Here, the word 저 (I) is both the topic of the sentence (talking about "I" here) and the subject of the sentence ("I" is the subject, and "am" is the verb").

51

In the following sentence, the topic marking particle is used twice, but only one word is the topic of the sentence while the other is the subject.

내일은 저는 일해요. = As for tomorrow, I work.
[nae-i-reun jeo-neun il-hae-yo.]

내일, "tomorrow", is followed by -은 and is the topic, not the subject, of the verb 일하다, "to
[nae-il]   [-eun]   [il-ha-da]
work", because it is not "tomorrow" that works, but rather "I" that work.

Subject marking particles : -이/가

The role of subject marking particles is relatively simple compared to the role of topic marking particles.

Track
17

> ### Conjugation
>
> **Word ending with a final consonant + -이**
>   [-i]
> **Word ending with a vowel + -가**
>   [-ga]

Ex)

이 책 = this book
[i chaek]
이 책 + 이 = 이 책이
[i chaek]   [i]   [i chae-gi]

가방 = bag
[ga-bang]
가방 + 이 = 가방이
[ga-bang]   [i]   [ga-bang-i]

학교 = school
[hak-kkyo]
학교 + 가 = 학교가
[hak-kkyo]   [ga]   [hak-kkyo-ga]

Fundamentally, topic marking particles (-은/는) express the topic of the sentence, and subject marking particles (-이/가) express the subject of the sentence. However, that is not everything!

What more is there about the particles -은/는/이/가?

(1)

In addition to marking topics, -은/는 has the nuance of "about" something, "as for" something, or even "unlike other things" or "different from other things".

Ex)

이거 = this / 사과 = apple / -예요 = to be / is
[i-geo]   [sa-gwa]   [-ye-yo]

이거 사과예요. = This is an apple.
[i-geo sa-gwa-ye-yo.]

Track 17

You can add -은/는 to this sentence. The subject is 이거, which ends in a vowel, so you would add -는.

이거는 사과예요. = (The other things are not apples, but) THIS is an apple.
[i-geo-neun sa-gwa-ye-yo.]

Imagine someone talking like this:

이거 커피예요. = This is coffee
[i-geo keo-pi-ye-yo.]

이거는 물이에요. = That was coffee, but THIS ONE, it is water.
[i-geo-NEUN mu-ri-e-yo.]

이거는 오렌지 주스예요. = And THIS ONE, it is different again, it is orange juice.
[i-geo-NEUN o-ren-ji ju-seu-ye-yo.]

이거는 뭐예요? = And as for this one, what is it?
[i-geo-NEUN mwo-ye-yo?]

As you can see from this example, -은/는 has the role of emphasizing the topic of the sentence by giving it the nuance of "that one is ..., and/but THIS ONE is...".

It is unnecessary to use -은/는 in every sentence because of this nuance, so try not to use it all the time unless you REALLY want to place an emphasis on the topic.

For example, if you want to say "The weather is nice today" in Korean, you can say it many ways:

1. 오늘 날씨 좋네요.
   [o-neul nal-ssi jon-ne-yo.]
   The weather is good today.

2. 오늘은 날씨 좋네요.
   [o-neu-reun nal-ssi jon-ne-yo.]
   The weather (has not been so good lately, but) today (it) is good.

3. 오늘 날씨는 좋네요.
   [o-neul nal-ssi-neun jon-ne-yo.]
   Today (everything else is not good, but at least) the weather is good.

Track 17

The examples above show how powerful and useful the topic marking particles (-은/는) can be in how your Korean sentence is understood!

(2)

In addition to marking subjects, -이/가 has the nuance of "none other than", "nothing but", [-i/ga] as well as marking the subject without emphasizing it too much when used in a complex sentence.

Let's say you are talking to someone, and he/she asks you "WHAT is good?" (emphasizing "what") by saying:

"뭐가 좋아요?"
[mwo-ga jo-a-yo?]

뭐 = what
[mwo]
가 = subject marking particle (because 뭐 ends in a vowel)
[ga]
좋아요 = good (from the verb 좋다, meaning "to be good")

You can reply to this question in several different ways:

책 = book
[chaek]

이 책 좋아요.
[i chaek jo-a-yo.]
This book is good.

(The simplest way to say something is good.)

**Track
17**

이 책은 좋아요.
[i chae-geun jo-a-yo.]
(The other books are not good, and I do not care about the other books, but at least) This

book is good.

이 책이 좋아요.
[i chae-gi jo-a-yo.]
There are no other books as good as this one.

In the last response, the sentence structure is:

이 (This) + 책 (book) + 이 (subject marking particle) + 좋아요 (good)
[i]   [chaek]   [i]   [jo-a-yo]

The subject marking particle 이 (or 가) emphasizes the subject (책) of the verb (좋아요).

This type of sentence structure can also be used when you are speaking with someone who

says "ABC 좋아요" (ABC is the subject here), but you want to express your opinion that
        [ABC jo-a-yo.]
XYZ (subject) is good, not ABC.

"ABC 좋아요? XYZ가 좋아요!"
[ABC jo-a-yo? XYZ-ga jo-a-yo!]

With -이/가, you can add more flavor and a more concrete meaning to your Korean sentence with an added emphasis on the subject without saying extra words to express what you mean as you would in English.

As you can see from the previous pages of this lesson, -은/는 and -이/가 have different roles. The role of -은/는 as a compare/contrast factor is much stronger than -이/가 because of how easily you can change the topic of a sentence with -은/는. However, when forming more complex sentences, such as "I think the book that you bought is more interesting than the book I bought", -은/는 is not commonly used. Often at times, -은/는/이/가 can be dropped unless particles are absolutely needed to clarify the meaning, in which -이/가 is used more often.

Track 17

Sample Dialogue

Track 18

A: 이거 복숭아예요?
[i-geo bok-ssung-a-ye-yo?]

B: 아니요. 그것은 사과예요.
[a-ni-yo. geu-geo-seun sa-gwa-ye-yo.]

A: 이것이 복숭아예요?
[i-geo-si bok-ssung-a-ye-yo?]

B: 네, 맞아요.
[ne, ma-ja-yo.]

A: *Is this a peach?*

B: *No. That's an apple.*

A: *Then, is THIS a peach?*

B: *Yes, that's right.*

* For ease of pronunciation, native Korean speakers often say
이거는 *instead of* **이것은** *and* **그거는** *instead of* **그것은.**

✎ Exercises for Lesson 9

1. What are the topic marking particles in Korean?

(   )   &   (   )

2. What are the subject marking particles in Korean?

(   )   &   (   )

3. Which of the following is incorrect?

     a. 이 차 + 은 / 는 = 이 차는
       [i cha]   [eun] [neun]   [i cha-neun]

     b. 가방 + 은 / 는 = 가방은
       [ga-bang]   [eun] [neun]   [ga-bang-eun]

     c. 이 책 + 이 / 가 = 이 책가
       [i chaek]   [i]   [ga]   [i chaek-ga]

     d. 학교 + 이 / 가 = 학교가
       [hak-kkyo]   [i]   [ga]   [hak-kkyo-ga]

4. If "이거 좋아요" means "This is good" in Korean, how do you say "I do not know about the
[i-geo jo-a-yo]
other things, but THIS ONE is good"?

(   )

5. Since "피자 비싸요" means "Pizza is expensive", how would you say "Other things are not
[pi-ja bi-ssa-yo]
expensive, but PIZZA is expensive"?

(   )

Check the answers on **p.160**

6. As mentioned, "피자 비싸요" means "Pizza is expensive", so when someone asks you
[pi-ja bi-ssa-yo]
"뭐가 비싸요?", how would you respond "It is the PIZZA that is expensive"?
[mwo-ga bi-ssa-yo?]

(   )

7. If "오늘 날씨 좋네요" means "Today, the weather is good", how would you say "Today, at least
[o-neul nal-ssi jon-ne-yo]
the weather is good (not necessarily anything else)"?

(   )

8. How do you say "What is this?" in polite/formal Korean?

(   )

9. How do you say "What is it that is good?" in polite/formal Korean?

(   )

10. Translate "What about this one? What is it?" to polite/formal Korean.

(   )

LESSON **10**

Have, Do not have, There is, There is not

있어요. 없어요.

Track 19

You will learn when and how to use the endings 있어요 and 없어요. You can use these endings when you talk about what people **HAVE/DO NOT HAVE**, in addition to things that **EXIST/DO NOT EXIST**.

있어요 comes from the verb 있다, which expresses that something "exists".
[i-sseo-yo]   [it-tta]

If you are talking about someone or something existing in a specific place, 있다 means "to be":

    Ex) I am here. / It is over there. / I am at home now.

If you are talking about something (or someone in some cases) in your possession, it means "to have":

    Ex) I have a sister. / I have eleven dogs. / Do you have a private airplane?

Sometimes, however, it can mean both. For example, the sentence "I have a sister" can be replaced by the sentence "There is a sister (in my family)" in Korean.

60

없어요 is the opposite, and it comes from the verb 없다. Even though there IS a way to
[eop-sseo-yo]　　　　　　　　　　　　　　　　　　　[eop-tta]

say the same thing by using 있어요 in a negative sentence, there is this independent verb in

Korean (없어요) for expressing non-existence. It is more convenient to use 없어요 rather

than saying 있지 않아요 or 안 있어요 (which will be covered in a future lesson).
　　　　　　[it-jji a-na-yo]　　[an i-sseo-yo]

So, in conclusion:

있어요 ⟷ 없어요
[i-sseo-yo]　　[eop-sseo-yo]

When you use 있어요/없어요 with other nouns, you have to put what you have or what you

do not have IN FRONT OF "있어요" or "없어요".
　　　　　　　　　　[i-sseo-yo]　　[eop-sseo-yo]

Track 19

Sample Sentences

물 있어요. = There is water. / Water exists. / I have water. / They have water.
[mul i-sseo-yo.]

물 있어요? = Is there water? / Do you have water? / Do they have water?
[mul i-sseo-yo?]

친구 있어요. = I have friends. / I have a friend. / There are friends.
[chin-gu i-sseo-yo.]

친구 있어요? = Do you have friends? / Do they have friends?
[chin-gu i-sseo-yo?]

시간 있어요. = There is time. / I have time. / They have time.
[si-gan i-sseo-yo.]

시간 있어요? = Is there time? / Do you have time? / Do they have time?
[si-gan i-sseo-yo?]

Just by replacing 있어요 with 없어요 you get sentences in the opposite meanings.
　　　　　　[i-sseo-yo]　　[eop-sseo-yo]

물 없어요 = There is no water. / I do not have water. / They do not have water.
[mul eop-sseo-yo.]

친구 없어요. = I do not have friends.
[chin-gu eop-sseo-yo.]

시간 없어요. = There is no time. / I do not have time. / We do not have time.
[si-gan eop-sseo-yo.]

Do you remember the usages of -은/는, the topic marking particles, and -이/가, the subject
[-eun/neun]   [-i/ga]
marking particles?

-은 and -는 mark the topic of a sentence, and at the same time emphasize the contrast
between the topic of the sentence and the other things.

If you say "시간은 있어요", people may think you have nothing but time, meaning that you
[si-ga-neun i-sseo-yo]
have no other resources, or that you have time but you do not want to spend any of that
time with them.

If you say 시간 없어요, it means "I do not have time" in the most neutral sense. However, if
[si-gan eop-sseo-yo]
you want to say "I have other things, but TIME is not what I have", you can simply add -은 to
[-eun]
the end of 시간, and the phrase becomes 시간은 없어요.
[si-gan]

Track 19

If someone asks you "What is it that you do not have?" or "What are you saying that you
do not have?", you can answer by saying 시간이 없어요, which means "TIME is what I do not
have".

있어요 and 없어요 can be used to form many interesting and frequently used expressions in
Korean. For example:

재미 = fun
[jae-mi]

재미 + 있어요 = 재미있어요

This literally means "fun exists", but it means "it is interesting"

* Notice how the two words are even written without any space in between. That is because it has already become an expression used daily.

Ex) TalkToMeInKorean 재미있어요!
[jae-mi-i-sseo-yo!]
= TalkToMeInKorean is fun! / TalkToMeInKorean is interesting!

Track 19

63

Sample Dialogue

Track
20

A: 경화 씨, 우산 있어요?
[gyeong-hwa ssi, u-san i-sseo-yo?]

B: 아니요, 없어요.
[a-ni-yo, eop-sseo-yo.]

A: 그럼 이것은요?
[geu-reom i-geo-seun-nyo?]

B: 그것은 석진 씨 거예요.
[geu-geo-seun seok-jjin ssi geo-ye-yo.]

A: Kyung-hwa, do you have an umbrella?

B: No, I don't.

A: Then, what is this?

B: That is Seokjin's.

* *For ease of pronunciation, native Korean speakers often say*
이거는 *instead of* **이것은** *and* **그거는** *instead of* **그것은**.

✎ *Exercises for Lesson 10*

1. Translate "to have" or "there is" to polite/ formal Korean.

(   )

2. How do you say "I have time" in polite/ formal Korean?

(   )

3. How would you say "I do not have time" in polite/formal Korean?

(   )

4. If you want to say "I have other things, but time is not what I have", how do you say this in Korean?

(   )

5. How do you ask someone "Do you have friends?" or "Do you have a friend?"

(   )

6. How do you ask someone "Do you have Korean friends?"

(   )

7. How do you say that you "do not have" something?

(   )

8. Let's imagine that you own a store. You have run out of bottled water and a customer is looking for some, so you want to tell him/ her, "We do not have water". How do you say this in Korean?

(   )

9. Do you remember the Korean word for "fun"? What is it?

(   )

10. How do you say that something "is no fun" or "is not interesting"?

(   )

Check the answers on **p.160**

BLOG

HAN RIVER
(한강)

한강 (The Han River) has become an iconic symbol of Seoul, and as the 4th longest river in Korea, it runs through a good portion of the country. The river is quite broad, and in Seoul, you can visit 12 recreational parks along its shorelines, participate in exciting 수상 스포츠 (water sports), take a bike ride along the 74 kilometer-long 자전거 도로 (bike lane), kick back and relax on the 한강 유람선 (Han River Cruise Ship), enjoy a 콘서트 (concert) by the water, or just hang out with friends and loved ones along the shore.

여름 날씨 (Summer weather) in Korea can be very hot and humid during the day, but at night, it cools off just enough to enjoy the night air. One of our favorite things to do in the summertime is to visit 한강 at sunset and hang out with 친구들 (friends). Not only are you able to take some AMAZING 사진 (pictures) of the river at this time, but you're also not working up a sweat trying to experience an important portion of Korean 역사 (history).

Congratulations!

You've made it past lesson 10!

You're nearly half way finished with Level 1!

화이팅!

LESSON 11

Please give me.

··· 주세요

In this lesson, let us look at how to ask "Do you have ...?" or "Is there ...?" and also how to say "Give me .... please" or "I would like to have ... please".

Do you remember how to say "I have ...", "You have ..." or "There is ..."?

있어요 = I have ... / You have ... / There is ...
[i-sseo-yo]
없어요 = I do not have ... / You do not have ... / There is not ...
[eop-sseo-yo]

Sample Sentences

사과 = apple
[sa-gwa]
사과 있어요. = I have an apple. / There are apples. / They have some apples.
[sa-gwa i-sseo-yo.]
사과 없어요. = I do not have an apple. / There is no apple.
[sa-gwa eop-sseo-yo.]

오렌지 = orange
[o-ren-ji]
오렌지 있어요. = I have an orange. / There are oranges. / They have some oranges.
[o-ren-ji i-sseo-yo.]
오렌지 없어요. = I do not have an orange. / There is no orange.
[o-ren-ji eop-sseo-yo.]

Now, if you want to ask whether someone has something or not, or whether something exists, simply raise the tone at the end of the sentence and you can make it a question.

있어요? = Do you have ...? / Is there ...?
[i-sseo-yo?]
없어요? = Don't you have ...? / There is not ...?
[eop-sseo-yo?]

Sample Sentences

사과 = apple
[sa-gwa]
사과 있어요. = I have an apple. / There are some apples.
[sa-gwa i-sseo-yo.]
사과 있어요? = Do you have an apple? / Do you have apples?
[sa-gwa i-sseo-yo?]
사과 없어요? = You do not have an apple? / There are no apples?
[sa-gwa eop-sseo-yo?]

시간 = time
[si-gan]
시간 있어요? = Do you have some time?
[si-gan i-sseo-yo?]
시간 없어요? = You do not have time?
[si-gan eop-sseo-yo?]

커피 = coffee
[keo-pi]
커피 있어요? = Do you have coffee?
[keo-pi i-sseo-yo?]
커피 없어요? = Don't you have coffee? You do not have coffee?
[keo-pi eop-sseo-yo?]

돈 = money
[don]
돈 있어요? = Do you have money?
[don i-sseo-yo?]
돈 없어요? = You do not have money?
[don eop-sseo-yo?]

Track 21

Now, after figuring out whether someone has something or not, you might as well want to ask for some of it, by saying "Please give me …" or "I would like to have … please".

주세요 = Please give me

주세요 comes from the verb 주다 which means "to give". 주세요 ONLY means "please give"
[ju-se-yo]   [ju-da]
in polite/formal language regardless of who said it or to whom it is said. Just say the name of the item you want + 주세요.

Sample Sentences

돈 주세요. = Please give me some money.
[don ju-se-yo.]
펜 주세요. = Please give me a pen.
[pen ju-se-yo.]
장갑 주세요. = Please give me (a pair of) gloves.
[jang-gap ju-se-yo.]

Track 21

Sample Conversations

A: 사과 있어요? = Do you have apples?
[sa-gwa i-sseo-yo?]
　　B: 네. 사과 있어요. = Yes, we have apples.
　　　[ne. sa-gwa i-sseo-yo.]
A: 사과 주세요. = Give me (an/some) apple(s).
[sa-gwa ju-se-yo.]

* Please note that there is no strict distinction between plural and singular in Korean nouns.

A: 커피 있어요? = Do you have coffee?
[keo-pi i-sseo-yo?]
　　B: 아니요. 커피 없어요. = No, we do not have coffee.
　　　[a-ni-yo. keo-pi eop-sseo-yo.]
A: 우유 있어요? = Do you have milk?
[u-yu i-sseo-yo?]
　　B: 네. 우유 있어요. = Yes, we have milk.
　　　[ne. u-yu i-sseo-yo.]
A: 우유 주세요. = Give me some milk, please.
[u-yu ju-se-yo.]

주세요 can be used in many different situations: when asking someone to hand something
[ju-se-yo]
over to you, when ordering something in a restaurant, when asking for an item in a shop, or

when attached to a verb (which you will learn how to do in a later lesson) to ask someone

to do something for you.

Sample Sentences

아이스크림 주세요. = Please give me some ice cream.
[a-i-seu-keu-rim ju-se-yo.]
햄버거 주세요. = Please give me a hamburger.
[haem-beo-geo ju-se-yo.]
김치 주세요. = Please give me some kimchi.
[gim-chi ju-se-yo.]
불고기 주세요. = Please give me some bulgogi.
[bul-go-gi ju-se-yo.]
밥 주세요. = Please give me rice. / Please give me food.
[bap ju-se-yo.]

**Track
21**

Sample Dialogue

A: 저기요! 여기 라자냐 없어요?
[jeo-gi-yo! yeo-gi la-ja-nya eop-sseo-yo?]

B: 네, 없어요. 죄송합니다.
[ne, eop-sseo-yo. joe-song-ham-ni-da.]

A: 그럼 이거 주세요.
[geu-reom i-geo ju-se-yo.]

B: 네, 알겠습니다.
[ne, al-get-sseum-ni-da.]

A: *Excuse me! You don't have lasagne here?*

B: *No, we don't. I'm sorry.*

A: *Then, I will have this.*

B: *Yes, sir/ma'am.*

✎ Exercises for Lesson 11

1. In Korean, 커피 means "coffee". How do you say "Do you have coffee?" in Korean?
[keo-pi]

(   )

2. How do you say "Yes, we have coffee" in Korean?

(   )

3. How do you translate "No, we do not have coffee." to Korean?

(   )

4. How do you say "Don't you have coffee?" or "You don't have coffee?" in Korean?

(   )

5. Write "Give me some milk, please" in Korean.

(   )

Check the answers on **p.160**

LESSON **12**

It is delicious, It tastes awful, Thank you for the food

맛있어요. 잘 먹겠습니다.

Track 23

In the previous lesson, we learned how to say "Please give me ..." or "I would like to have ... please" in Korean. Do you remember the expression?

주세요 = Please give me ... / I would like to have ...
[ju-se-yo]

You can also use this expression (주세요) to order something in a restaurant or to ask for more side dishes while you are eating.

김밥 주세요. = Kimbap, please (when ordering in a restaurant).
[gim-bap ju-se-yo.]
불고기 주세요. = Bulgogi, please (when ordering in a restaurant).
[bul-go-gi ju-se-yo.]
김치 주세요. = Please give us some kimchi here.
[gim-chi ju-se-yo.]

In this lesson, you will learn how to say "It tastes good" and "It is delicious" as well as how to thank someone for a meal or food before and after eating.

75

맛 = taste

맛 means "taste" in Korean. Now, do you remember how to say "there is" or "I have"? 있어요 is
[mat]   [i-sseo-yo]
the expression. So by putting 맛 and 있어요 together, you get the expression 맛있어요, which
                                                                            [ma-si-sseo-yo]
means "It is delicious".

맛있어요. = It is tasty. / It is delicious.

Sample Sentences

이거 맛있어요. = This is delicious.
[i-geo ma-si-sseo-yo.]

저 케이크 맛있어요. = That cake is delicious.
[jeo ke-i-keu ma-si-sseo-yo.]

삼겹살 맛있어요. = Samgyupsal is delicious.   * 삼겹살 = pork belly
[sam-gyeop-ssal ma-si-sseo-yo.]

치킨 맛있어요. = Chicken is delicious.
[chi-kin ma-si-sseo-yo.]

뭐가 맛있어요? = What is delicious?
[mwo-ga ma-si-sseo-yo?]

Track 23

Now, do you also remember how to say "there is not" or "I do not have" in Korean? Yes, 없어요
                                                                                     [eop-sseo-yo]
is the expression. So by putting 맛 and 없어요 together, you get the expression 맛없어요, which
                                                                              [ma-deop-sseo-yo]
means "It does not taste good".

맛없어요. = It is not tasty. / It is not delicious. / It tastes awful.

Note that the pronunciation of the last letter in 맛, which is ㅅ, changes according to the word
that follows it. When it is NOT followed by any word, it is pronounced as [t], ending the word
there. When it is followed by 있어요, it becomes an [s] sound, making 맛있어요 pronounced
as [ma-si-sseo-yo]. When it is followed by 없어요, it becomes a [d] sound, making 맛없어요
pronounced as [ma-deop-sseo-yo].

76

Sample Sentences

이거 맛없어요? = Does this taste awful?
[i-geo ma-deop-sseo-yo?]

이 차 맛없어요. = This tea tastes awful.
[i cha ma-deop-sseo-yo.]

굴 맛없어요. = Oysters taste awful.
[gul ma-deop-sseo-yo.]

Now, you know how to say "It is delicious" and "It is not delicious". It is time to learn phrases that you can say to give thanks for a meal before and after you eat it. This is very important, especially if someone is treating you or if you are invited to someone's house.

잘 먹겠습니다.

Track 23

잘 먹겠습니다 literally means "I am going to eat well" or "I will eat well" (Don't worry about
[jal meok-kke-sseum-ni-da.]
the grammar that is used here yet. Just learn this as a set phrase for the time being). This expression is used frequently among Koreans when they are about to start eating a meal regardless of who is paying for the meal. However, in the case someone in particular is paying for the meal, the other(s) will say "잘 먹겠습니다" to the person who is paying. When you eat with your friends with whom you do not use polite/formal language, and when you want to joke that your friend should buy you food, you can say 잘 먹을게! which implies that you
[jal meo-geul-kke!]
are thanking them because they are going to treat you.

잘 먹었습니다.

Once you have finished the meal and you want to thank someone for the meal, or just give thanks for the meal in general, you can use 잘 먹었습니다. This phrase literally means "I have
[jal meo-geo-sseum-ni-da]
eaten well" (again, don't worry about the grammar here). Nevertheless, what it really means is "Thank you for the food".

Sample Dialogue

A: 저 치킨 맛있어요?
[jeo chi-kin ma-si-sseo-yo?]

B: 네.
[ne.]

A: 저거 주세요.
[jeo-geo ju-se-yo.]

B: 여기 있습니다.
[yeo-gi it-sseum-ni-da.]

A: 감사합니다. 잘 먹겠습니다.
[gam-sa-ham-ni-da. jal meok-kke-sseum-ni-da.]

A: Is that chicken over there tasty?

B: Yes.

A: I will have that.

B: Here you are, sir/ma'am.

A: Thank you. I will enjoy the meal.

🖉 Exercises for Lesson 12

1. How do you say "taste" or "flavor" in Korean?

(   )

2. Your friend invites you to dinner and cooks for you. The food is really good! How will you tell your friend that "it is tasty" or "it is delicious" in Korean?

a. 맛있어요.
[ma-si-sseo-yo.]

b. 맛없어요.
[ma-deop-sseo-yo.]

c. 죄송해요.
[joe-song-hae-yo.]

3. How do you say "it is not tasty" or "it is not delicious" in Korean?

a. 맛있어요.

b. 맛없어요.

c. 죄송해요.

4. Your friend has invited you to his house and he cooked for you. In order to thank him for the meal, you want to say a certain Korean expression before you eat. This Korean expression is said aloud very frequently just before eating a meal. How do you say this expression in Korean?

(   )

5. You have finished your meal, the food was great, and you want to thank your friend for the meal. The phrase you can say literally means "I have eaten well", but it really means "thank you for the food". How do you say that in Korean?

(   )

Check the answers on **p.160**

LESSON 13

I want to ···

-고 싶어요

Track 25

In this lesson, you will learn how to say "I want to..." in Korean.

In the previous lesson, we learned how to say that something is delicious, as well as how to give thanks for the food you are going to eat or have eaten already.

맛있어요. = It is delicious.
[ma-si-sseo-yo.]
맛없어요. = It is not tasty.
[ma-deop-sseo-yo.]
잘 먹겠습니다. = Thank you for the food. / I will enjoy it.
[jal meok-kke-sseum-ni-da.]
잘 먹었습니다. = I enjoyed the meal. / Thanks for the food.
[jal meo-geo-sseum-ni-da.]

Before you order something in a restaurant or in a coffee shop, you might as well ask your friends what they want to eat or drink, and also tell them what you want to have.

In English, you add the expression "want to" before the verb, but in Korean, you need to change the end of the verb. Don't worry. It is not too difficult to do.

-고 싶어요 = I want to + V

Now, let's practice. Here are some frequently used Korean verbs:

가다 = to go
[ga-da]
보다 = to see
[bo-da]
먹다 = to eat
[meok-tta]

> ## Conjugation
>
> ## Verb stem + -고 싶어요

Track 25

Ex)

to go = 가다 → 가 + -고 싶어요 → 가고 싶어요.
[ga-da]

가고 싶어요. = I want to go.
[ga-go si-peo-yo.]

to see = 보다 → 보 + -고 싶어요 → 보고 싶어요.
[bo-da]

보고 싶어요. = (lit. I want to see/look/watch.) I miss you.
[bo-go si-peo-yo.]

to eat = 먹다 → 먹 + -고 싶어요 → 먹고 싶어요.
[meok-tta]

먹고 싶어요. = I want to eat.
[meok-kko si-peo-yo.]

Sample Conversations

A: 뭐 먹고 싶어요? = What do you want to eat?
[mwo meok-kko si-peo-yo?]
　　B: 햄버거 먹고 싶어요. = I want to eat a hamburger.
[haem-beo-geo meok-kko si-peo-yo.]

A: 뭐 먹고 싶어요? = What do you want to eat?
[mwo meok-kko si-peo-yo?]
   B: 회 먹고 싶어요. = I want to eat raw fish.
[hoe meok-kko si-peo-yo.]

Here is another useful word to know:

$$더 = more$$

Now that you know how to say "I want to eat (it)" you can say "I want to eat more" using

this word 더.
[deo]

Sample Sentences

Track 25

먹고 싶어요. = I want to eat it.
[meok-kko si-peo-yo.]
더 먹고 싶어요. = I want to eat more.
[deo meok-kko si-peo-yo.]

주세요. = Please give me.
[ju-se-yo.]
더 주세요. = Please give me more.
[deo ju-se-yo.]

Sample Dialogue

Track
26

A: 아이스크림 먹고 싶어요.
[a-i-seu-keu-rim meok-kko si-peo-yo.]

B: 집에 아이스크림 없어요.
[ji-be a-i-seu-keu-rim eop-sseo-yo.]

A: 있어요.
[i-sseo-yo.]

B: 진짜요?
[jin-jja-yo?]

A: I would like to eat ice cream.

B: There is no ice cream at home.

A: There is.

B: Really?

✎ Exercises for Lesson 13

1. There are many delicious types of food in Korea, so it is hard to choose just one dish for lunch. You may want to order the same thing as one of your friends just to make things easier. In that case, how do you say "What do you want to eat?" in Korean?

( )

2. If the food was really great, you may want to eat more. How can you ask for more food in Korean?

( )

Match the words with the related sentence.

3. 영화 (movie)
[yeong-hwa]

4. 여행 (trip)
[yeo-haeng]

5. 피자 (pizza)
[pi-ja]

a. 먹고 싶어요.
[meok-kko si-peo-yo]

b. 보고 싶어요.
[bo-go si-peo-yo]

c. 가고 싶어요.
[ga-go si-peo-yo]

LESSON **14**

What do you want to do?

뭐 -고 싶어요?

In our previous lesson, we learned how to say "I want to" in Korean. In this lesson, we will practice using the structure "I want to" in context through more sample conversations.

First, let's look at five verbs which are very commonly used in Korean. Don't worry if they are new to you. At this point, knowing how to use them is more important than memorizing each and every one of them.

하다 = to do
[ha-da]
보다 = to see
[bo-da]
먹다 = to eat
[meok-tta]
사다 = to buy
[sa-da]
마시다 = to drink
[ma-si-da]

* If you look up a verb in a Korean dictionary, you will see every verb ending in the form "-다". "-다" is the basic form of all Korean verbs, so all the Korean verbs that you find in a dictionary will be "-다".

85

Do you remember how to change a verb into the "I want to + verb" form?

하 + (-다) + -고 싶어요

Yes. -다 disappears and you add -고 싶어요 after the verb.
[-da]   [-go si-peo-yo]

하다 → 하고 싶어요 = I want to do ...
[ha-go si-peo-yo]

보다 → 보고 싶어요 = I want to see ...
[bo-go si-peo-yo]

먹다 → 먹고 싶어요 = I want to eat ...
[meok-kko si-peo-yo]

사다 → 사고 싶어요 = I want to buy ...
[sa-go si-peo-yo]

마시다 → 마시고 싶어요 = I want to drink ...
[ma-si-go si-peo-yo]

Track 27

Do you remember how to say "WHAT" in Korean?

뭐 = what

Sample Conversations

* Remember: In Korean, objects come before verbs.

A: 뭐 하고 싶어요? = What do you want to do?
[mwo ha-go si-peo-yo?]

    B: 텔레비전 보고 싶어요. = I want to watch TV.
[tel-le-bi-jeon bo-go si-peo-yo.]

A: 텔레비전 보고 싶어요? = You want to watch TV?
[tel-le-bi-jeon bo-go si-peo-yo?]

    B: 네. = Yeah.
[ne.]

A: 뭐 보고 싶어요? = What do you want to watch?
[mwo bo-go si-peo-yo?]

    B: 뉴스 보고 싶어요. = I want to watch the news.
[nyu-sseu bo-go si-peo-yo]

A: 이거 사고 싶어요. = I want to buy this.
[i-geo sa-go si-peo-yo.]

    B: 이거요? = This one?
[i-geo-yo?]

A: 네. 이거 먹고 싶어요. = Yeah. I want to eat this.
[ne. i-geo meok-kko si-peo-yo.]
　　　B: 이거 뭐예요? = What is this?
[i-geo mwo-ye-yo?]
A: 이거 김밥이에요. = This is kimbap.
[i-geo gim-ppa-bi-e-yo.]

Sample Sentences

읽다 = to read
[ik-tta]
읽고 싶어요. = I want to read.
[il-kko si-peo-yo.]

자다 = to sleep
[ja-da]
자고 싶어요. = I want to sleep.
[ja-go si-peo-yo.]

놀다 = to hang out, to play
[nol-da]
놀고 싶어요. = I want to play.
[nol-go si-peo-yo.]

Track 27

쉬다 = to rest
[swi-da]
쉬고 싶어요. = I want to rest.
[swi-go si-peo-yo.]

일하다 = to work
[il-ha-da]
일하고 싶어요. = I want to work.
[il-ha-go si-peo-yo.]

영화 보다 = to watch a movie
[yeong-hwa bo-da]
영화 보고 싶어요. = I want to watch a movie.
[yeong-hwa bo-go si-peo-yo.]

김밥 먹다 = to eat kimbap
[gim-bap meok-tta]
김밥 먹고 싶어요. = I want to eat kimbap.
[gim-bap meok-kko si-peo-yo.]

Sample Dialogue

A: 뭐 마시고 싶어요?
[mwo ma-si-go si-peo-yo?]

B: 콜라 마시고 싶어요.
[kol-la ma-si-go si-peo-yo.]

A: 콜라 없어요.
[kol-la eop-sseo-yo.]

B: 그럼 사이다 주세요.
[geu-reom sa-i-da ju-se-yo.]

A: *What would you like to drink?*

B: *I would like to drink coke.*

A: *There is no coke.*

B: *Then, I will have cider [a clear carbonated beverage such as Sprite or 7-UP].*

✏ Exercises for Lesson 14

Fill in the blanks to make the Korean sentences and the English sentences have the same meaning.

A: 저거 ¹·(　　　　　) 싶어요.
　　= I want to read that one.

　　B: 이거요?
　　　　= This one?

A: 아니요. ²·(　　　　　)요.
　　= No. That one over there.

　　B: 이거요?
　　　　= This one?

A: 네, ³·(　　　　)요.
　　= Yes, that one.

　　B: 이거 ⁴·(　　　　)예요?
　　　　= What is this?

A: 그거 ⁵·(　　　　)이에요.
　　= That is a book.

Check the answers on **p.161**

89

LESSON 15

Sino-Korean Numbers

일, 이, 삼, 사, …

Track
29

In this lesson, you will learn about 숫자 (numbers)! We wish we could say that there is a very
[sut-jja]

easy way to learn Korean numbers once and never forget them, but the truth is, there is

not. As far as numbers are concerned, you will have to keep practicing using them until they

stick. There are two systems of numbers in Korean: native Korean numbers and sino-Korean

numbers. In this lesson, we will introduce sino-Korean numbers up to 1,000. We will get

into native Korean numbers in another lesson.

Sino-Korean numbers

We will use the term "sino-Korean" when a Korean word is based on the Chinese language.

Since Korea has received a lot of influence from China, many words in the Korean language

have their roots in the Chinese language. So over the course of time, Korean people started

using both the sino-Korean number system and the native Korean number system. The situations and contexts in which each system is used are different, but don't worry. You will get used to the two systems and how to differentiate between these two by practicing with us!

1 일
[il]

2 이
[i]

3 삼
[sam]

4 사
[sa]

You may have heard of the Korean superstition about the number four being unlucky. The word for "four" in Korean, 사, has the same sound as the sino-Korean word for "death". This is the reason why there is an "F" button in an elevator in Korea instead of a "4" button!

Track 29

5 오
[o]

6 륙 or 육
[ryuk]   [yuk]

The Korean word for the number six can change spelling depending on whether it is at the beginning or in the middle of a word. When saying 육 on its own, it is just 육. If you say "five six", or 오륙, the ㄹ is added. Somewhere throughout the course of history, Korean people decided that 오륙 was more natural to say than 오육.

7 칠
[chil]

8 팔
[pal]

9 구
[gu]

10 십
[sip]

91

From numbers 11 and through to 99, the rest is easy! Just think of it as a simple math equation using the numbers 일 through 십 (If you do not like math or are not good at math, don't freak out! It truly is very simple!)

For example:

11 = 십 (10) + 일 (one)
[sip]   [il]

25 = 이 (two) + 십 (10) + 오 (five)
[i]   [sip]   [o]

33 = 삼 (three) + 십 (10) + 삼 (three)
[sam]   [sip]   [sam]

99 = 구 (nine) + 십 (10) + 구 (nine)
[gu]   [sip]   [gu]

100 백
[baek]

1,000 천
[cheon]

Track 29

Can you guess how to say 312 in Korean?

Yes, you are right.

THREE + HUNDRED + TEN + TWO

삼 + 백 + 십 + 이
[sam] [baek] [sip] [i]

Ex)

1,234 = 1,000 (천) + 2 (이) + 100 (백) + 3 (삼) + 10 (십) + 4 (사)

512 = 5 (오) + 100 (백) + 10 (십) + 2 (이)

Note that for 1,000, 100, and 10, you do not have to say one (일) + thousand (천), 일백, or 일십.

How to say ZERO

Zero is either 영 or 공. When counting to 10 in Korean, you can say 영일이삼사오륙칠팔구십 or 공일이삼사오륙칠팔구십 for 0, 1, 2, 3, 4, 5, 6, 7, 8, 9, 10.

Sample Dialogue

Track 30

A: TV 보고 싶어요.
[ti-beu-i bo-go si-peo-yo.]

B: 몇 번이요?
[myeot beo-ni-yo?]

A: 11번이요.
[si-bil-beo-ni-yo.]

B: 12번이요?
[si-bi-beo-ni-yo?]

A: 아니요. 11번이요.
[a-ni-yo. si-bil-beo-ni-yo.]

A: I would like to watch TV.

B: What channel?

A: Channel 11.

B: Channel 12?

A: No. Channel 11.

93

✏ *Exercises for Lesson* 15

Do you remember the sino-Korean numbers? Let's practice!

1. How do you count from 1 to 10 using the sino-Korean number system?

( )

2. How do you say the number "**476**" in Korean?

( )

Check the answers on **p.161**

3. In what year were the Vancouver Winter Olympic Games held? How do you say that year in Korean?

( )

4. A McDonald's Big Mac meal set is ₩**4,900** in Korea. How do you say "₩**4,900**" in Korean?

( )

* ₩ = 원
[won]

5. How do you say "zero" in Korean?

( )

LESSON **16**

Basic Present Tense

-아/어/여요

Track 31

In this lesson, you will learn how to conjugate Korean verbs into present tense form. When you look up Korean verbs in a dictionary, they are in the infinitive form:

가다 = to go
[ga-da]

먹다 = to eat
[meok-tta]

자다 = to sleep
[ja-da]

때리다 = to hit
[ttae-ri-da]

웃다 = to laugh
[ut-tta]

* *Note that all verbs end with* -다 *at the end.*
[-da]

You need to change these verbs into more realistic, more natural and more flexible forms.

When you are conjugating verbs into any tense (past, present, future, etc.), the first thing you need to do is drop the -다 since you almost never need it. With the -다 dropped, you are left with the "verb stem".

So, the verb stems of the previous verbs introduced are as follows:

가
[ga]
먹
[meok]
자
[ja]
때리
[ttae-ri]
웃
[ut]

To these, you add the appropriate verb endings to make them complete. In this lesson we are going to learn how to change these dictionary forms of the verbs into the present tense.

In order to conjugate a verb into the present tense, you take the verb stem, and add one of these endings:

Track 31

-아요

-어요

-여요

* Note that we are introducing the endings in polite language. Don't worry about learning to use different politeness levels yet. Once you have learned how to say everything in polite language, changing it to other politeness levels is very easy to do.

Conjugation

1) If the verb stem's last vowel is ㅏ or ㅗ, it is followed by 아요.
[a]   [o]   [a-yo]

2) If the last vowel is NOT ㅏ or ㅗ, it is followed by 어요.
[a]   [o]   [eo-yo]

3) Only one verb stem, which is 하, is followed by 여요.
[ha]   [yeo-yo]

Sample Sentences

1. 가다 = to go
    [ga-da]
    The verb stem is 가, and the last vowel is ㅏ, so you add 아요. It first becomes 가
    [ga]   [a]   [a-yo]
    + 아요, and then more naturally, it becomes 가요 for ease of pronunciation.
                                              [ga-yo]

    가다 = to go (dictionary form)
    [ga-da]
    → 가요 = I go. / You go. / He goes. / She goes. / They go.
      [ga-yo]

2. 먹다 = to eat
    [meok-tta]
    The verb stem is 먹 and the last vowel is ㅓ, NOT ㅏ or ㅗ, so you add 어요. This
                     [meok]   [eo]   [eo-yo]
    becomes 먹 + 어요

    먹다 = to eat (dictionary form)
    [meok-tta]
    → 먹어요 = I eat. / You eat. / He eats. / etc.
      [meo-geo-yo]
    * Note that there is consonant assimilation here: 먹 + 어 sounds like 머거.
                                                     [meok + eo]   [meo-geo]

3. 보다 = to see, to watch, to look
    [bo-da]
    Verb stem? 보
              [bo]
    What is it followed by? 아요
                           [a-yo]
    보 + 아요 → Over time, it started being pronounced and written as 봐요.
                                                                    [bwa-yo]
    (Say 보 + 아 + 요 three times as fast.)

    보다 = to see, to watch, to look
    [bo-da]
    → 봐요 = I see. / I look. / I watch. / You look. / etc.
      [bwa-yo]

4. 보이다 = to be seen, to be visible
    [bo-i-da]
    Verb stem? 보이
              [bo-i]
    What is it followed by? 어요
                           [eo-yo]
    보이 + 어요 → 보여요
                [bo-yeo-yo]

97

보이다 = to be seen, to be visible
[bo-i-da]

→ 보여요 = I see it. / It is visible.
[bo-yeo-yo]

5. 하다 = to do
[ha-da]

Verb stem? 하
[ha]

What is it followed by? 여요
[yeo-yo]

하 + 여요 → 하여요
[ha-yeo-yo]

Over time, 하여요 became → 해요
[hae-yo]

* Here, please just remember that the verb 하다 is very versatile. You can add a noun in front of it and you can form new verbs with it.

Track 31

studying = 공부 to study = 공부하다
[gong-bu] [gong-bu-ha-da]

cleaning (the room) = 청소 to clean = 청소하다
[cheong-so] [cheong-so-ha-da]

cooking = 요리 to cook = 요리하다
[yo-ri] [yo-ri-ha-da]

We will introduce how to do this in lesson number 22. For now, just remember that 하다 becomes 해요 in the present tense, and it means "I do", "You do", "He does", or "They do".

Q: Are there any irregularities or exceptions?

A: Sadly, yes, there are, but don't worry. Even those exceptions are NOT too far away from the regular rules!! Of course, we will introduce them in the nicest and easiest way possible through our future lessons. Thank you once again for studying with us through this book!

98

Sample Dialogue

Track
32

A: 이 아파트 살아요?
[i a-pa-teu sa-ra-yo?]

B: 네.
[ne.]

A: 몇 호 살아요?
[myeot ho sa-ra-yo?]

B: 708호요.
[chil-baek-pa-ro-yo.]

A: *Do you live in this apartment?*

B: *Yes.*

A: *What is your room number?*

B: *Room 708.*

✏️ Exercises for Lesson 16

In order to conjugate a verb into the present tense, take the verb stem and add one of the following endings: 아요, 어요, *or* 여요.
[a-yo]   [eo-yo]   [yeo-yo]

Choose an ending from the choices above to match the description below:

1. If the verb stem's last vowel is ㅏ or ㅗ, it is followed by (   ).
[a]   [o]

2. Only one verb stem, which is 하, is followed by (   ).
[ha]

3. If the last vowel is NOT ㅏ or ㅗ, it is followed by (   ).
[a]   [o]

4. "To eat" is 먹다 in Korean. Write the present tense conjugation of 먹다 in Korean.
[meok-tta]

(   )

5. If "to do" is 하다 in Korean, how would you write the present tense conjugation of this verb so
[ha-da]
it means "I do"?

(   )

LESSON **17**

Past Tense

-았/었/였어요

In the previous lesson, we looked at the basic way of conjugating the verbs in the infinitive form into the present tense form. Do you remember how?

Track 33

Conjugation

Verb stems ending with vowels ㅗ or ㅏ are followed by -아요.
[o]   [a]   [-a-yo]

Verb stems ending with vowels OTHER THAN ㅗ or ㅏ are followed by -어요.
[-eo-yo]

Verb stem 하 is followed by -여요.
[-yeo-yo]

Great! Now let's learn how to conjugate verbs into the past tense.

If you understand how to change verbs into the present tense, understanding how to change them into the past tense is just as easy. A similar rule is applied to making past tense sentences, and the endings are as follows:

-았어요

-었어요

-였어요

You can add those to the verb stems, or you can think of it as just replacing the "요" at the end of present tense sentences with -ㅆ어요.

Conjugation

Verb stems ending with vowels ㅗ or ㅏ are followed by **-았어요.**
[o]　　[a]　　　　　　　　　　　　　　　　[-a-sseo-yo]

Verb stems ending with vowels other than ㅗ or ㅏ are followed by **-었어요.**
[-eo-sseo-yo]

Verb stem 하 is followed by **-였어요.**
[-yeo-sseo-yo]

Track 33

1) 사다 = to buy
[sa-da]

Verb stem　　　= 사
[sa]

* *Drop the final* -다 *from the verb to get the verb stem.*
[da]

Past tense　　　= 사 + 았어요
[sa + a-sseo-yo]

　　　　　　　= 샀어요
[sa-sseo-yo]

　　　　　　　= I bought / you bought / s/he bought / they bought / etc.

2) 오다 = to come
[o-da]

Verb stem　　　= 오
[o]

Past tense　　　= 오 + 았어요
[o + a-sseo-yo]

　　　　　　　= 왔어요
[wa-sseo-yo]

　　　　　　　= I came / you came / s/he came / they came / we came / etc.

3) 적다 = to write down
[jeok-tta]

Verb stem   = 적
[jeok]

Past tense   = 적 + 었어요
[jeok + eo-sseo-yo]

                 = 적었어요
[jeo-geo-sseo-yo]

                 = I wrote / you wrote / s/he wrote / they wrote / we wrote / etc.

4) 하다 = to do
[ha-da]

Verb stem   = 하
[ha]

Past tense   = 하 + 였어요
[ha + yeo-sseo+yo]

                 = 했어요
[hae-sseo-yo]

                 = I did / you did / he did / they did / etc.

Sample Sentences

Track 33

먹다 (Verb stem = 먹) = to eat
[meok-tta]   [meok]
Present Tense: 먹어요
[meo-geo-yo]
Past Tense: 먹었어요
[meo-geo-sseo-yo]

잡다 (Verb stem = 잡) = to catch
[jap-tta]   [jap]
Present Tense: 잡아요
[ja-ba-yo]
Past Tense: 잡았어요
[ja-ba-sseo-yo]

팔다 (Verb stem = 팔) = to sell
[pal-da]   [pal]
Present Tense: 팔아요
[pa-ra-yo]
Past Tense: 팔았어요
[pa-ra-sseo-yo]

놀다 (Verb stem = 놀) = to play, to hang out
[nol-da]   [nol]
Present Tense: 놀아요
[no-ra-yo]

Past Tense: 놀았어요
[no-ra-sseo-yo]

쓰다 (Verb stem = 쓰) = to write, to use
[sseu-da]   [sseu]
Present Tense: 써요 (NOT 쓰어요)
[sseo-yo]
Past Tense: 썼어요
[sseo-sseo-yo]

기다리다 (Verb stem = 기다리) = to wait
[gi-da-ri-da]   [gi-da-ri]
Present Tense: 기다려요 (NOT 기다리어요)
[gi-da-ryeo-yo]
Past Tense: 기다렸어요
[gi-da-ryeo-sseo-yo]

이상하다 (Verb stem = 이상하) = to be strange
[i-sang-ha-da]   [i-sang-ha]
Present Tense: 이상해요 (NOT 이상하여요)
[i-sang-hae-yo]
Past Tense: 이상했어요
[i-sang-hae-sseo-yo]

Track 33

멋있다 (Verb stem = 멋있) = to be cool, to be awesome
[meo-si-tta]   [meo-sit]
Present Tense: 멋있어요
[meo-si-sseo-yo]
Past Tense: 멋있었어요
[meo-si-sseo-sseo-yo]

There are some other things that are more important to learn before the future tense in Level 1.

So we are going to introduce those things in the rest of the lessons for Level 1, and we will introduce the future tense in Level 2. Please be patient!

Sample Dialogue

Track 34

A: 잘 먹었습니다.
[jal meo-geo-sseum-ni-da.]

B: 맛있었어요?
[ma-si-sseo-sseo-yo?]

A: 네, 정말 맛있었어요. 감사합니다.
[ne, jeong-mal ma-si-sseo-sseo-yo. gam-sa-ham-ni-da.]

A: Thank you for the meal.

B: Was it good?

A: Yes, it was really good. Thank you.

✎ Exercises for Lesson 17

In order to conjugate a verb into the past tense, add one of the following endings to the verb stem:

았어요, **었어요**, or **였어요**.
[a-sseo-yo] [eo-sseo-yo] [yeo-sseo-yo]

Fill in the blanks below.

Check the answers on **p.161**

1. 팔다 = to sell
[pal-da]

　　Present Tense: (　　　　　　　　)　Past Tense: 팔았어요
[pa-ra-sseo-yo]

2. 이상하다 = to be strange
[i-sang-ha-da]

　　Present Tense: 이상해요　　　Past Tense: (　　　　　　　)
[i-sang-hae-yo]

3. 기다리다 = to wait
[gi-da-ri-da]

　　Present Tense: 기다려요　　　Past Tense: (　　　　　　　)
[gi-da-ryeo-yo]

4. 쓰다 = to write, to use
[sseu-da]

　　Present Tense: (　　　　　　)　Past Tense: 썼어요
[sseo-sseo-yo]

5. 멋있다 = to be cool, to be awesome
[meo-si-tta]

　　Present Tense: 멋있어요　　　Past Tense: (　　　　　　)
[meo-si-sseo-yo]

LESSON **18**

Location Marking Particles

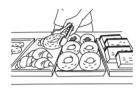

어디, -에, -에서

In Korean, as you already know, there are particles which are used to mark the roles of some nouns. So far, you have learned about subject marking particles (-이 and -가) and topic marking particles (-은 and -는). In this lesson, you will learn about the location marking particles, -에 and -에서, and also how to say WHERE in Korean.

[-i]   [-ga]
[-eun]   [-neun]
[-e]   [-e-seo]

Track 35

First let's learn the word for "WHERE" or "WHICH PLACE".

어디 = where, which place

Here, although the word "어디" is romanized as "eo-di", please make sure that your pronunciation of the second letter "디" is not actually "di", but rather like a voiced "th" sound (ex. "th" as in "there"). You can accomplish this by placing your tongue between your upper and lower teeth, but don't force a constant stream of air over your tongue and through your teeth. The standard romanization system that the Korean government uses for "디" is not "thi", but the actual pronunciation is closer to "thi". We are using "di" here, so please make sure that you are not pronouncing the word "어디" as "eo-di", but rather as "eo-thi".

Now, let's look at how to ask someone "Where do you want to go?" in Korean.

to go = 가다
[ga-da]
to want to = -고 싶어요
[-go si-peo-yo]

Do you remember how to form a sentence using -고 싶어요? Yes, you drop the letter "-다" at the end of a verb and attach -고 싶어요 after that.
[-go si-peo-yo]

가다 + -고 싶어요 → 가고 싶어요 = I want to go.

Track 35

가고 싶어요 = I want to go.

가고 싶어요? = Do you want to go?

Now, you just add the word 어디 in front of the verb.
[eo-di]
어디 가고 싶어요? = Where do you want to go?
[eo-di ga-go si-peo-yo?]

Q: Why use location marking particles?

A: Whereas it is POSSIBLE to make sentences without location marking particles (as in the example above: 어디 가고 싶어요?), by using the right location marking particles, you can make your message very clear. There are many location marking particles in Korean, but let us look at the two most basic particles, -에 and -에서.
[-e]   [-e-seo]

-에 = at, to, in

Conjugation

Noun + -에
[-e]

-에 is a location marking particle, but it is not only used to mark locations. It means "at", "to"
[-e]
and so on, and it can be used to mark a location, a time, a situation, and many other things.

However, here, let us just focus on its role of marking locations. Let us look at how it is used

inside a Korean sentence, by looking at some sample sentences.

Sample Sentences

Track 35

1. Let's say "I went to school." in Korean.

   to go = 가다
   [ga-da]

   I went = 가 + 았어요 = 갔어요
   [ga-sseo-yo]

   school = 학교
   [hak-kkyo]

   to = -에
   [-e]

   I went to school. = 학교에 갔어요.
   [hak-kkyo-e ga-sseo-yo.]

2. Let's say "I came to Korea." in Korean.

   to come = 오다
   [o-da]

   I came = 오 + 았어요 = 왔어요
   [wa-sseo-yo]

   Korea = 한국
   [han-guk]

   to = -에
   [-e]

   I came to Korea. = 한국에 왔어요.
   [han-gug-e wa-sseo-yo.]

3. Let's say "Where do you want to go?" in Korean.

to go = 가다
[ga-da]

do you want to go = 가 + 고 싶어요 = 가고 싶어요
[ga-go si-peo-yo]

where = 어디
[eo-di]

to = -에
[-e]

Where do you want to go? = 어디에 가고 싶어요?
[eo-di-e ga-go si-peo-yo?]

4. Let's say "Where are you?" in Korean.

to be = 있다
[it-tta]

are you = 있 + 어요 = 있어요
[i-sseo-yo]

where = 어디
[eo-di]

at = -에
[-e]

Where are you? = 어디에 있어요?
[eo-di-e i-sseo-yo?]

Where are you now? = 지금 어디에 있어요?
[ji-geum eo-di-e i-sseo-yo?]

어디에 있어요 지금?
[eo-di-e i-sseo-yo ji-geum?]

-에서 = at, in, from

> ### *Conjugation*
> ## Noun + -에서
> [-e-seo]

-에서 can express many things, but here let's look at two of its main roles.

-에서 expresses:

1) a location where an action is taking place

(ex. I studied in the library. / I met my friends in Seoul.)

2) the meaning of "from" a place

   (ex. I came from Seoul. / This package came from Spain.)

Ex)

사무실 = workroom, office

사무실에 = to the office, to an office, to my office

사무실에서 = from the office, from an office, from my office

The difference between -에 and -에서

-에 and -에서 can both be translated to "at" in English. How are they different then?

Track 35

-에 expresses a location where something "is" or "exists", or a direction that you are going toward.

Ex)

집에 있어요. = I am at home.
[ji-be i-sseo-yo.]
집에 가요. = I am going home.
[ji-be ga-yo.]
사무실에 있어요. = I am at the office.
[sa-mu-si-re i-sseo-yo.]

-에서 expresses a location where an action is taking place.

Ex)

집에서 일해요. = I work at home.
[ji-be-seo il-hae-yo.]
집에서 뭐 해요? = What are you doing at home?
[ji-be-seo mwo hae-yo?]
사무실에서 일해요. = I work at the office.
[sa-mu-si-re-seo il-hae-yo.]

Here are some incredibly useful verbs and conjugations:

가다 = to go
[ga-da]
가요 = I go / you go / s/he goes / they go / let's go
[ga-yo]
갔어요 = went / to have gone
[ga-sseo-yo]

오다 = to come
[o-da]
와요 = I come / you come / s/he comes / they come / let's come
[wa-yo]
왔어요 = came / to have come
[wa-sseo-yo]

있다 = to be / to exist
[it-tta]
있어요 = there is / there are / I have / you have / they have
[i-sseo-yo]
있었어요 = was / to have been
[i-sseo-sseo-yo]

Track 35

보다 = to see
[bo-da]
봐요 = I see / they see / you see / we see / let's see
[bwa-yo]
봤어요 = saw / to have seen
[bwa-sseo-yo]

하다 = to do
[ha-da]
해요 = I do / they do / you do / we do / let's do
[hae-yo]
했어요 = did / to have done
[hae-sseo-yo]

Sample Dialogue

🎤
**Track
36**

A: 지금 어디 있어요?
[ji-geum eo-di i-sseo-yo?]

B: 사무실에 있어요.
[sa-mu-si-re i-sseo-yo.]

A: 저 지금 빵집에 있어요. 빵 먹고 싶어요?
[jeo ji-geum ppang-jji-be i-sseo-yo. ppang meok-kko
si-peo-yo?]

B: 네. 슈크림 빵 먹고 싶어요.
[ne. syu-keu-rim ppang meok-kko si-peo-yo.]

A: *Where are you now?*

B: *I am in the office.*

A: *I am at the bakery. Would you like some
bread?*

B: *Yes, I would like to eat some cream puffs.*

✏ *Exercises for Lesson 18*

1. How do you say "where" or "which place" in Korean?

(   )

에 *and* 에서
[e]   [e-seo]
Choose the location particle that best fits each sentence.

2. 집(   ) 있어요.

= I am at home.

3. 집(   ) 뭐 해요?

= What are you doing at home?

4. 집(   ) 일해요.

= I work at home.

5. 집(   ) 가요.

= I am going home.

LESSON 19

When

언제

In this lesson, you will learn how to say WHEN in Korean. You will also get some practice with answering questions such as "when did you do it?", "when did you arrive?", "when did you come?", etc.

Track 37

언제 = when

Unlike 어디, to which you have to add location marking particles to specify, 언제 can always
[eo-di]   [eon-je]
be used on its own. Let's try using the word 언제 in context.

1) "When did you do (it)?"

when = 언제
[eon-je]
you did (it) = 하다 + 였어요 = 했어요
[hae-sseo-yo]
did you do (it)? = 했어요?
[hae-sseo-yo?]
When did you do it? = 언제 했어요?
[eon-je hae-sseo-yo?]

115

2) "When did you arrive?"

to arrive = 도착하다
[do-cha-ka-da]

you arrived = 도착했어요
[do-cha-kae-sseo-yo]

did you arrive? = 도착했어요?
[do-cha-kae-sseo-yo?]

When did you arrive? = 언제 도착했어요?
[eon-je do-cha-kae-sseo-yo?]

3) "When did you come?"

to come = 오다
[o-da]

you came = 왔어요
[wa-sseo-yo]

did you come? = 왔어요?
[wa-sseo-yo?]

When did you come? = 언제 왔어요?
[eon-je wa-sseo-yo?]

4) "When do you get up?"

Track 37

to get up = 일어나다
[i-reo-na-da]

you get up = 일어나요
[i-reo-na-yo]

do you get up? = 일어나요?
[i-reo-na-yo?]

When do you get up? = 언제 일어나요?
[eon-je i-reo-na-yo?]

5) "When/what time do you get up in the morning?"

morning = 아침
[a-chim]

in the morning = 아침에
[a-chi-me]

In the morning, when do you get up? = 아침에 언제 일어나요?
[a-chi-me eon-je i-reo-na-yo?]

at what time = 몇 시에
[myeot si-e]

What time do you get up in the morning? = 아침에 몇 시에 일어나요?
[a-chi-me myeot si-e i-reo-na-yo?]

Here are some additional words to use when someone asks the question "언제?"

오늘 = today
[o-neul]

어제 = yesterday
[eo-je]

내일 = tomorrow
[nae-il]

지금 = now
[ji-geum]

아까 = earlier (today), a while ago (today)
[a-kka]

나중에 = later
[na-jung-e]

Track 37

Sample Dialogue

Track
38

A: 석진 씨는 집에 갔어요.
[seok-jjin ssi-neun ji-be ga-sseo-yo.]

B: 언제 갔어요?
[eon-je ga-sseo-yo?]

A: 방금 전에 갔어요.
[bang-geum jeo-ne ga-sseo-yo.]

A: Seokjin went home.

B: When did he go?

A: He just left.

✏ *Exercises for Lesson 19*

Let's practice by using the word that means "when" in Korean, 언제.
[eon-je]

1. How do you say "When did you do (it)?" in Korean?

( )

2. How do you say "When do you get up?" in Korean?

( )

3. How do you say "When did you come?" in Korean?

( )

4. How do you say "When did you arrive?" in Korean?

( )

5. How do you say "At what time do you get up in the morning?" in Korean?

( )

Check the answers on **p.161**

LESSON **20**

Native Korean Numbers

하나, 둘, 셋, 넷, ...

Track 39

In Lesson 15, we introduced some sino-Korean numbers:

일 = one
[il]

이 = two
[i]

삼 = three
[sam]

사 = four
[sa]

오 = five
[o]

육 = six
[yuk]

칠 = seven
[chil]

팔 = eight
[pal]

구 = nine
[gu]

십 = ten
[sip]

백 = hundred
[baek]

120

천 = thousand
[cheon]

만 = ten thousand, and so on.
[man]

Now let's have a look at some native Korean numbers. There are cases where sino-Korean numbers are used, cases where native Korean numbers are used, and there are also some cases where both sino-Korean numbers and native Korean numbers are used together.

1) When you tell the time, you have to use native Korean numbers to say the hours and sino-Korean numbers to say the minutes.

2) When you say your age in everyday conversations, you use native Korean numbers. However, in some very formal settings like in the court of law or in a formal report, sino-Korean numbers are used to express your age.

Track 39

3) When you are counting years, you can use either sino-Korean numbers or native Korean numbers. However, the words that you use for counting the years change depending on whether you use sino-Korean numbers or native Korean numbers.

Q: So how do you determine which number system to use in which situation?

A: You do not have to try to, and you cannot really generalize the usages of the two different number systems. It is best to just learn to use the different number systems along with the fitting context.

Now, let us go over the native Korean numbers and practice saying how old we are.

121

Native Korean numbers

1 하나
[ha-na]

2 둘
[dul]

(You need to pronounce this word 둘 by placing your tongue between your upper and lower teeth,

not behind your upper teeth.)

3 셋
[set]

(It is not as strong as the English word "set".)

4 넷
[net]

5 다섯
[da-seot]

6 여섯
[yeo-seot]

7 일곱
[il-gop]

8 여덟
[yeo-deol]

9 아홉
[a-hop]

10 열
[yeol]

Track 39

From 11 to 19 is simple. You just put the number 10 and add another number after it.

Ex)

열 (10) + 하나 (1) = 열하나 (11)
[yeol-ha-na]

열 (10) + 다섯 (5) = 열다섯 (15)
[yeol-da-seot]

열 (10) + 아홉 (9) = 열아홉 (19)
[yeo-ra-hop]

The same rule as previously mentioned for 11 through 19 applies to 21-29, 31-39, 41-49, and so on.

20 스물
[seu-mul]

30 서른
[seo-reun]

40 마흔
[ma-heun]

50 쉰
[swin]

60 예순
[ye-sun]

70 일흔
[il-heun]

80 여든
[yeo-deun]

90 아흔
[a-heun]

Track 39

Now, here is an interesting piece of information.

From numbers 1 through 99, the usage of native Korean numbers is generally very distinctively different from the usage of sino-Korean numbers. However, for bigger units like 100, 1,000, 10,000 and so on, the words for these bigger units in the native Korean numbers are no longer used, and only sino-Korean numbers are now used.

So, 100 as the sino-Korean number is 백, and even when you need to use the native Korean number, you use the same word.
[baek]

When you want to say 101, 102, and so on, you need to combine the systems together.

101 = 백 (sino-Korean) + 하나 (native Korean)
[baek / 100]   [ha-na / 1]

205 = 이 (sino-Korean) + 백 (sino-Korean) + 다섯 (native Korean)
[i / 2]   [baek / 100]   [da-seot / 5]

123

Let us have a look at how to talk about age.

There are two ways of saying your age, but here, let's look at the more ordinary and everyday usage.

You say a native Korean number and add 살 after it.
[sal]
However, the numbers 1, 2, 3, 4, and 20 change forms before a noun:

1 하나 → 한 살
[ha-na]   [han sal]

2 둘 → 두 살
[dul]   [du sal]

3 셋 → 세 살
[set]   [se sal]

4 넷 → 네 살
[net]   [ne sal]

…

Track 39

20 스물 → 스무 살
[seu-mul]   [seu-mu sal]

21 스물하나 → 스물한 살
[seu-mul-ha-na]   [seu-mul-han sal]

…

The following are examples from age 1 through 100 in native Korean numbers, followed by the age counter 살:
[sal]

한 살 (1), 두 살, 세 살, 네 살, 다섯 살, 여섯 살, 일곱 살, 여덟 살, 아홉 살, 열 살 (10), 열한 살 (11), 열두 살, 열세 살, 열네 살, 열다섯 살, 열여섯 살, 열일곱 살, 열여덟 살, 열아홉 살, 스무 살 (20), 스물한 살 (21), 스물두 살, 스물세 살, 스물네 살, 스물다섯 살, 스물여섯 살, 스물일곱 살, 스물여덟 살, 스물아홉 살, 서른 살 (30), 서른한 살 (31), 서른두 살, 서른세 살, 서른네 살, 서른다섯 살, 서른여섯 살, 서른일곱 살, 서른여덟 살, 서른아홉 살, 마흔 살 (40), 마흔한 살 (41), 마흔두 살, 마흔세 살, 마흔네 살, 마흔다섯 살, 마흔여섯 살, 마흔일곱 살, 마흔여덟 살,

마흔아홉 살, 쉰 살 (50), 쉰한 살(51), 쉰두 살, 쉰세 살, 쉰네 살, 쉰다섯 살, 쉰여섯 살, 쉰일곱 살, 쉰여덟 살, 쉰아홉 살, 예순 살 (60), 예순한 살 (61), 예순두 살, 예순세 살, 예순네 살, 예순다섯 살, 예순여섯 살, 예순일곱 살, 예순여덟 살, 예순아홉 살, 일흔 살 (70), 일흔한 살 (71), 일흔두 살, 일흔세 살, 일흔네 살, 일흔다섯 살, 일흔여섯 살, 일흔일곱 살, 일흔여덟 살, 일흔아홉 살, 여든 살 (80), 여든한 살 (81), 여든두 살, 여든세 살, 여든네 살, 여든다섯 살, 여든여섯 살, 여든일곱 살, 여든여덟 살, 여든아홉 살, 아흔 살 (90), 아흔한 살 (91), 아흔두 살, 아흔세 살, 아흔네 살, 아흔다섯 살, 아흔여섯 살, 아흔일곱 살, 아흔여덟 살, 아흔아홉 살, 백 살 (100)

Did you find your age?

To say "I am ## years old", say the age + 이에요.
[i-e-yo]

Track 39

Sample Sentences

한 살이에요.   I am one year old.
[han sa-ri-e-yo.]

열 살이에요.   I am ten years old.
[yeol sa-ri-e-yo.]

스무 살이에요.   I am twenty years old.
[seu-mu sa-ri-e-yo.]

서른 살이에요.   I am thirty years old.
[seo-reun sa-ri-e-yo.]

Sample Dialogue

Track 40

A: 몇 살이에요?
[myeot sa-ri-e-yo?]

B: 스물여섯 살이에요.
[seu-mul-lyeo-seot sa-ri-e-yo.]

A: 저는 스물다섯 살이에요.
[jeo-neun seu-mul-da-seot sa-ri-e-yo.]

A: How old are you?

B: I am 26 years old.

A: I am 25 years old.

✏ Exercises for Lesson *20*

Check the answers on **p.161**

Do you remember the native Korean numbers? Here is a short review:

1 = 하나   2 = 둘   3 = 셋   4 = 넷   5 = 다섯   6 = 여섯   7 = 일곱   8 = 여덟
[ha-na]   [dul]   [set]   [net]   [da-seot]   [yeo-seot]   [il-gop]   [yeo-deol]

9 = 아홉   10 = 열
[a-hop]   [yeol]

Write the following numbers and phrases using native Korean numbers:

1. 20

(   )

6. I am **27** years old.

(   )

2. I am **eleven** years old.

(   )

7. I am **29** years old.

(   )

3. I am **twenty** years old.

(   )

8. I am **forty** years old.

(   )

4. I am **24** years old.

(   )

9. I am **fifty** years old.

(   )

5. I am **twenty-five** years old.

(   )

10. I am **52** years old.

(   )

127

BLOG

TAKING
A TAXI

We're not saying this because we are biased, but Korea has some of the best public transportation in the world. Okay, so maybe we are just a *wee* bit biased, but when it comes to public transit, Korea knows what's up! Whether you want to take KTX, the subway, a bus, or a taxi, it's all reasonably priced and efficiently gets you from A to B without having to own or rent a car.

택시(Taxis) are everywhere in Seoul: some are equipped with WiFi (which is totally and completely AWESOME, by the way), some are geared toward foreigners, and some are just a simple cab. Generally speaking, 택시 are clean, safe, comfortable, and best of all, relatively cheap depending on where you want to go. As of 2015년 5월 (May 2015), the base fare in Seoul for 일반 택시 (standard taxis — the silver ones with a blue or green stripe on the side) is 3,000 won for the first 2 kilometers, and it increases by 100 won every 142 meters beyond the initial 2 kilometers. Most 택시 now accept T-money cards, credit and debit

cards, and good ol' paper money. There will be a sign somewhere on or in the cab that says "카드 택시" (card taxi) to let you know that payment by card is possible.

There are actually a few other popular types of 택시 in Korea besides 일반 택시.

Many of the bright orange cabs you see on the street are "International" taxis. You can spot them easily because of the letters "Int'l" written on the side of the cab's top light. This means the drivers have been trained to speak multiple languages, albeit Chinese, English, and Japanese as they are the most frequently spoken aside from Korean, and the cost is the same as the 일반 택시. There are also some 모범 택시 (luxury taxis) that cost a little bit more, but more on that in a minute. If you'd like to reserve an international taxi so you don't have to wait for one, you can call by phone or do it online!

모범 택시 are black with a yellow sign on top of the car and are generally found in larger cities. This type of taxi is more expensive than the standard taxi (almost twice as much!), but if you want to be driven around by a driver that acts more like a chauffeur than a cabbie, then 모범 is a great choice! This cab is easily reserved if you're staying at a luxury hotel and want to go somewhere. All you have to do is ask the concierge to call you a cab and, more than likely, you will step into a 모범. If you feel like taking another type of cab, just walk a few feet away from your hotel to hail one.

Hailing a cab in Seoul is pretty simple: you can just stick your arm out horizontally, or stand next to a 택시 정류장 (taxi stand). Unoccupied cabs are identified by the bright red light in the front window that reads 빈차 (vacant car), and luckily, getting a cab in Seoul is fairly easy... except if you are trying to get a 택시 between midnight and 1 a.m. If you want, you can put your hands in the air and wave 'em like you just don't care to get a cab at this hour, but it's a lot less work to just stick your arm out and be patient :D

Taking a 택시 in an unfamiliar city is sometimes intimidating, especially if there is a dizzying array of options to choose from, but whichever taxi you choose to use in order to make your way around, make sure you look out the window and enjoy the view wherever you go! You can learn a lot about a place just by watching!

We hope that this blog post helped you learn a little more about riding a 택시 in Seoul.

Until next time!

Prices and information mentiond are gathered from Seoul metropolitan area. 택시 may be different in other parts of Korea.

LESSON **21**

Negative Sentences

안, -지 않다

Track 41

In this lesson, you will learn how to create negative sentences in Korean. There are two main ways to accomplish this:

(1) Add **안** before a verb

(2) Use the negative verb ending, **-지 않다**

Method (1) is simpler and more colloquial, and method (2) is relatively formal but not necessarily only for formal situations. If you want to use method (1), and add **안** before a verb, it is easier than method (2) because you do not have to worry about the different tenses of your sentences. The word **안** does not change the tense.

> ### *Conjugation*
>
> 가다 = to go
> [ga-da]
>
> 집에 가요. I am going home. / I go home.
> [ji-be ga-yo.]

132

집에 안 가요. I am NOT going home. / I DO NOT go home.
[ji-be an ga-yo.]
집에 안 가요? You are NOT going home? / You DO NOT go home?
[ji-be an ga-yo?]

버리다 = to throw away
[beo-ri-da]

그거 버렸어요. I threw it away.
[geu-geo beo-ryeo-sseo-yo.]
그거 안 버렸어요. I DID NOT throw it away.
[geu-geo an beo-ryeo-sseo-yo.]
그거 아직 안 버렸어요. I DID NOT throw it away yet.
[geu-geo a-jik an beo-ryeo-sseo-yo.]

-지 않다 is the basic form and you need to conjugate it according to the tense, too.
[-ji an-ta]

Present tense: -지 않아요
[-ji a-na-yo]
Past tense: -지 않았어요
[-ji a-na-sseo-yo]

**Track
41**

Conjugation

가다 = to go
[ga-da]
가지 않다 = to not go
[ga-ji an-ta]
가지 않아요 = I DO NOT go. / I am NOT going.
[ga-ji a-na-yo]
가지 않았어요 = I DID NOT go.
[ga-ji a-na-sseo-yo]

버리다 = to throw away
[beo-ri-da]
버리지 않다 = to not throw away
[beo-ri-ji an-ta]
버리지 않아요 = I DO NOT throw it away.
[beo-ri-ji a-na-yo]
버리지 않았어요 = I DID NOT throw it away.
[beo-ri-ji a-na-sseo-yo]

Sample Conversations

A: 아파요? = Does it hurt?
[a-pa-yo?]
    B: 안 아파요. = It does not hurt.
    [an a-pa-yo.]
A: 안 아파요? 진짜 안 아파요? = It does not hurt? It really does not hurt?
[an a-pa-yo? jin-jja an a-pa-yo?]
    B: 안 아파요. = It does not hurt.
    [an a-pa-yo.]

A: 안 먹어요? = You are not going to eat?
[an meo-geo-yo?]
    B: 안 먹어요! = I am not eating!
    [an meo-geo-yo!]
A: 정말 안 먹어요? 맛있어요! = You are really not going to eat? It is delicious.
[jeong-mal an meo-geo-yo? ma-si-sseo-yo!]
    B: 안 먹어요. 배 안 고파요. = I am not eating. I am not hungry.
    [an meo-geo-yo. bae an go-pa-yo.]

A: 이거 매워요? = Is this spicy?
[i-geo mae-wo-yo?]
    B: 아니요. 안 매워요. = No. It is not spicy.
    [a-ni-yo. an mae-wo-yo.]
A: 진짜 안 매워요? = It is really not spicy?
[jin-jja an mae-wo-yo?]
    B: 네. 안 매워요. = No, it is not spicy.
    [ne. an mae-wo-yo.]

Track 41

* There are two words which do not follow these rules that we just introduced. This is because they have antonyms that are very frequently used.

있다 = to be, exist; to have
[it-tta]
없다 = to not be, not exist; to not have
[eop-tta]

알다 = to know
[al-da]
모르다 = to not know
[mo-reu-da]

Sample Dialogue

A: 돈은 어디 있어요?
[do-neun eo-di i-sseo-yo?]

B: 현우 씨가 안 줬어요?
[hyeo-nu ssi-ga an jwo-sseo-yo?]

A: 네, 안 줬어요.
[ne, an jwo-sseo-yo.]

A: Where is the money?

B: Didn't Hyunwoo give you some?

A: No, he didn't.

✏ Exercises for Lesson 21

Do you remember how to make negative sentences in Korean? Let's practice!

1. 아프다 = to hurt   Write "it does not hurt" in Korean.
[a-peu-da]

(   )

2. If 버리다 means "to throw away" in Korean, how would you say "I threw it away" in Korean?
[beo-ri-da]

(   )

3. How do you say "I DID NOT throw it away" in Korean?

(   )

Fill in the blanks with a Korean word to make the Korean and English sentences have the same meaning.

A: 이거 매워요?
= Is this spicy?
B: 아니요. *4.* (   )
= No. It is not spicy.

ㄱ: 한국어 공부했어요?
= Did you study Korean?
ㄴ: 아니요. *5.* (   )
= No. I did not study Korean.

LESSON 22

Verbs

하다

So far, you have learned how to conjugate verbs from their infinitive form into the present

tense (현재 시제) and the past tense (과거 시제). You have also learned that 하다 has a
[hyeon-jae si-je]   [gwa-geo si-je]   [ha-da]

unique way of being conjugated, so let's practice conjugating 하다 verbs!

Track 43

하다 = to do

Do you remember how to conjugate 하다?

> ### Conjugation
>
> Dictionary form = 하다
>
> Present tense = 하 + 여요 = 해요
> [hae-yo]
>
> Past tense = 하 + 였어요 = 했어요
> [hae-sseo-yo]

It was previously mentioned that 하다 is a very powerful and useful word because it can be

combined with nouns to create verbs.

137

Many of the Korean nouns that indicate or describe an action or behavior can be combined with 하다 so they become verbs.

Noun	Infinitive Form	Present Tense	Past Tense
공부 = studying	공부하다 = to study	공부해요	→ 공부했어요
일 = work, job	일하다 = to work	일해요	→ 일했어요
기억 = memory	기억하다 = to remember	기억해요	→ 기억했어요
청소 = cleaning	청소하다 = to clean	청소해요	→ 청소했어요
요리 = cooking, dish	요리하다 = to cook	요리해요	→ 요리했어요
이사 = moving	이사하다 = to move, to move into a different house	이사해요	→ 이사했어요
노래 = song	노래하다 = to sing	노래해요	→ 노래했어요
노력 = effort	노력하다 = to make an effort, to try hard	노력해요	→ 노력했어요
동의 = agreement, agreeing	동의하다 = to agree	동의해요	→ 동의했어요
인정 = admitting, acknowledgement	인정하다 = to admit	인정해요	→ 인정했어요
후회 = regret	후회하다 = to regret	후회해요	→ 후회했어요
운동 = exercise	운동하다 = to exercise, to work out	운동해요	→ 운동했어요
사랑 = love	사랑하다 = to love	사랑해요	→ 사랑했어요
말 = words, language	말하다 = to speak	말해요	→ 말했어요
생각 = thought, idea	생각하다 = to think	생각해요	→ 생각했어요

Track 43

138

Making negative sentences with 하다 verbs

In order to make negative sentences using these 하다 verbs (check out Lesson 21 to recap on how to make negative sentences in Korean), you need to separate the noun part and the 하다 part and add 안 in between.

생각하다 → 생각 안 하다
노력하다 → 노력 안 하다

If you remember from Lesson 21, there are two ways to make negative sentences in Korean: adding 안 before the verb and using the verb ending 지 않다. If you want to use 지 않다 with 하다 verbs, you simply conjugate 하다 to 하지 않다.
[ha-da]   [ha-ji an-ta]

Track 43

139

Sample Dialogue

A: 청소했어요?
[cheong-so-hae-sseo-yo?]

B: 네.
[ne.]

A: 거실은요?
[geo-si-reun-nyo?]

B: 거실은 안 했어요.
[geo-si-reun an hae-sseo-yo.]

A: Have you cleaned up?

B: Yes.

A: How about the living room?

B: I didn't clean the living room.

✐ Exercises for Lesson 22

Match the English translation to the Korean word with the same meaning.

1. to clean

a. 노력하다
[no-ryeo-ka-da]

2. to exercise, to work out

b. 기억하다
[gi-eo-ka-da]

3. to regret

c. 청소하다
[cheong-so-ha-da]

4. to remember

d. 운동하다
[un-dong-ha-da]

5. to make an effort, to try hard

e. 후회하다
[hu-hoe-ha-da]

Check the answers on **p.162**

LESSON 23

Who?

누구?

Track
45

In this lesson, let's take a look at how to use the word for "who" in context, as well as how the form changes when the word 누구 is used as the subject in the sentence.

누구 = who

Remember the subject markers and the topic markers?

Subject markers: 이 / 가
[i]   [ga]
Topic markers: 은 / 는
[eun] [neun]

Subject markers emphasize the subject and show "who" did something, or "what" is being described, and topic markers emphasize the topic of your sentence and show "what" or "whom" you are talking about.

When you want to ask simple questions like "Who did it?" "Who helped her?" or "Who

made it?", you are emphasizing the subject, which is the word "who" here, so you need to use the subject marker 이 or 가.
[i] [ga]

누구 ends in a vowel so it would have to be followed by 가, but "누구" plus "가" changes to "누가" instead of "누구가" for ease of pronunciation.

> ## *Conjugation*
> 누구 = who
> [nu-gu]
> 누구 + 가 = 누구가 → 누가
> [nu-gu] [ga] [nu-ga]

Remember that this is ONLY when you are emphasizing "who" as the subject of an action or state.

Track 45

Ex)

1) When you want to ask "Who is it?" in Korean, you literally say "it is WHO?" so it becomes:

누구 (who) + 예요 (is) = 누구예요?
[nu-gu-ye-yo?]

2) When you want to ask "(Among these people, none other than) WHO is Jane?" you can say:

누구 (who) + 가 (subject marker) + 제인 (Jane) + 이에요? (is?)
= 누가 제인이에요?
[nu-ga je-i-ni-e-yo?]

3) When you want to ask "Who did it?":

누구 (who) + 가 (subject marker) + 했어요? (did?)
= 누가 했어요?
[nu-ga hae-sseo-yo?]

Sample Sentences

누가 전화했어요? = Who called?
[nu-ga jeo-nwa-hae-sseo-yo?]

이 사람은 누구예요? = Who is this? (This is who?)
[i sa-ra-meun nu-gu-ye-yo?]

어제 누가 왔어요? = Who came yesterday?
[eo-je nu-ga wa-sseo-yo?]

그거 누가 만들었어요? = Who made that?
[geu-geo nu-ga man-deu-reo-sseo-yo?]

누가 샀어요? = Who bought it?
[nu-ga sa-sseo-yo?]

Track 45

Sample Dialogue

Track
46

A: 누구였어요?
[nu-gu-yeo-sseo-yo?]

B: 동생이었어요.
[dong-saeng-i-eo-sseo-yo.]

A: 동생이 있었어요? 몰랐어요.
[dong-saeng-i i-sseo-sseo-yo? mol-la-sseo-yo.]

A: Who was it?

B: It was my younger brother/sister.

A: You have a younger brother/sister?
  I didn't know that.

✎ Exercises for Lesson 23

1. How do you say "who" in Korean?

(   )

Please fill in the blanks with **"누구"** *or* **"누가"**.

2. 어제 (   ) 왔어요?

   = Who came yesterday?

3. 이거 (   ) 예요?

   = Who is this?

4. 어제 (   ) 만났어요?

   = Who did you meet yesterday?

5. 그거 (   ) 만들었어요?

   = Who made that?

Check the answers on **p.162**

146

LESSON 24

Why? How?

왜? 어떻게?

Track 47

Through some of the previous lessons, you learned how to say "what", "where", "when", and "who" in Korean.

What = 뭐
[mwo]

Where = 어디
[eo-di]

When = 언제
[eon-je]

Who = 누구
[nu-gu]

In this lesson, you will learn two more 의문사 (interrogatives) to help you ask questions in
[ui-mun-sa]
Korean.

How = 어떻게

Why = 왜

How much (money) = 얼마

How + adjective/adverb = 얼마나

Generally, these interrogatives in Korean are used before the verb of a sentence. However, as the word order of the sentences is much more flexible (thanks, in part, to the subject/topic/object markers), they can come in at various parts of sentences, depending on the context or the nuance.

Sample Sentences

Track 47

1. 어떻게 = how
   [eo-tteo-ke]

   어떻게 찾았어요? = How did you find it?   (찾다 = to find, to look for)
   [eo-tteo-ke cha-ja-sseo-yo?]
   어떻게 왔어요? = How did you get here?   (오다 = to come)
   [eo-tteo-ke wa-sseo-yo?]

2. 왜 = why
   [wae]

   왜 전화했어요? = Why did you call?   (전화하다 = to call)
   [wae jeo-nwa-hae-sseo-yo?]
   왜 안 왔어요? = Why didn't you come?   (오다 = to come)
   [wae an wa-sseo-yo?]

3. 얼마 = how much
   [eol-ma]

   얼마예요? = How much is it?
   [eol-ma-ye-yo?]
   이거 얼마예요? = How much is this?
   [i-geo eol-ma-ye-yo?]
   저거 얼마예요? = How much is that?
   [jeo-geo eol-ma-ye-yo?]

148

그거 얼마예요? = How much is the thing that is near you but far from me?
[geu-geo eol-ma-ye-yo?]

얼마 냈어요? = How much did you pay?   (내다 = to pay)
[eol-ma nae-sseo-yo?]

4.   얼마나 + adjective/adverb = how + [often/fast/early/soon/etc.]
[eol-ma-na]

얼마나 자주 와요? = How often do you come?   (자주 = often / 오다 = to come)
[eol-ma-na ja-ju wa-yo?]

얼마나 커요? = How big is it?   (크다 = to be big)
[eol-ma-na keo-yo?]

얼마나 무거워요? = How heavy is it?   (무겁다 = to be heavy)
[eol-ma-na mu-geo-wo-yo?]

Track 47

Sample Dialogue

Track
48

A: 얼마나 기다렸어요?
[eol-ma-na gi-da-ryeo-sseo-yo?]

B: 많이 안 기다렸어요.
[ma-ni an gi-da-ryeo-sseo-yo.]

A: 죄송해요.
[joe-song-hae-yo.]

B: 아니에요.
[a-ni-e-yo.]

A: How long did you wait?

B: I didn't wait for long.

A: I am sorry.

B: It's okay.

✎ Exercises for Lesson 24

Match the English translation to the Korean word with the same meaning.

1. why

2. what

3. who

4. where

5. how

a. 누구
[nu-gu]

b. 어떻게
[eo-tteo-ke]

c. 왜
[wae]

d. 뭐
[mwo]

e. 어디
[eo-di]

Check the answers on **p.162**

Please fill in the blanks with "얼마" or "얼마나".

6. (﹚ 였어요? = How much was it?

7. (﹚ 자주 와요? = How often do you come?

8. (﹚ 무거워요? = How heavy is it?

9. (﹚ 예요? = How much is it?

10. (﹚ 커요? = How big is it?

LESSON 25

From A To B, From C Until D

-에서/부터 -까지

Track 49

In this lesson, you will learn how to say "from A to B" when talking about locations and "from A until B" when talking about time.

When directly translated to English, -에서 and -부터 mean "from", and -까지 means "to" or "until".
[-e-seo]　　　[-bu-teo]　　　　　　　　　[-kka-ji]

-에서 and -부터 may translate to English as the same word, but -에서 is more associated
[-e-seo]　　[-bu-teo]
with locations and -부터 is associated with time. Typically, these words are interchangeable in Korean, but there are certain cases where they are NOT interchangeable because of their associations.

Like all the other particles, -부터, -에서, and -까지 are used AFTER a noun or a pronoun, not BEFORE one.

"From A" in Korean is **"A에서"** or **"A부터"**

1. From Seoul

= 서울에서 (from Seoul to another place)
[seo-u-re-seo]
= 서울부터 ("starting from Seoul")
[seo-ul-bu-teo]

2. From now

= 지금부터
[ji-geum-bu-teo]
= 지금에서 (x)

3. From (or since) yesterday

= 어제부터
[eo-je-bu-teo]
= 어제에서 (x)

Track 49

Now, "to B" or "until B" in Korean is **"B까지"**

1. (From somewhere else) to Seoul = 서울까지
[seo-ul-kka-ji]
2. Until now = 지금까지
[ji-geum-kka-ji]
3. Until tomorrow = 내일까지
[nae-il-kka-ji]
4. Until when = 언제까지
[eon-je-kka-ji]

Sample Sentences

1.   From here to there

= 여기에서 저기까지

= 여기부터 저기까지

2. From Seoul to Busan

    = 서울에서 부산까지

    = 서울부터 부산까지

3. From head to toe

    = 머리부터 발끝까지

    = 머리에서 발끝까지

4. From morning until evening

    = 아침부터 저녁까지

    = 아침에서 저녁까지 (x)

Track 49

Sample Dialogue

A: 이 책은 처음부터 끝까지 정말
재미있어요.
[i chae-geun cheo-eum-bu-teo kkeut-kka-ji
jeong-mal jae-mi-i-sseo-yo.]

B: 언제 읽었어요?
[eon-je il-geo-sseo-yo?]

A: 주말에 읽었어요.
[ju-ma-re il-geo-sseo-yo.]

B: 어디에서 읽었어요?
[eo-di-e-seo il-geo-sseo-yo?]

A: 집에서 읽었어요.
[ji-be-seo il-geo-sseo-yo.]

A: This book is really interesting from
the beginning to the end.

B: When did you read it?

A: I read it over the weekend.

B: Where did you read it?

A: I read it at home.

✎ Exercises for Lesson 25

Do you remember how to say "*from point A to point B*" *or* "*until C to D*" *(in terms of time) by using* -에서/-부터+까지*? Let's practice how to use this sentence structure!*

1. -에서 and -부터 both mean "from" and they are usually interchangeable, but in some cases they are NOT interchangeable. For which one of the following is it interchangeable?

    a. From Seoul

    b. From now

    c. From yesterday

Write the following phrases in Korean using -에서/-부터 + 까지.

2. Until now

    (   )

3. Until tomorrow

    (   )

4. From here to there

    (   )

5. From head to toe

( )

6. From morning until evening

( )

7. From Seoul to Busan

( )

8. From yesterday until now

( )

9. Until when?

( )

10. From what time until when?

( )

Check the answers on **p.162**

ANSWERS
for Level 1, Lessons 1 ~ 25

Answers for Level 1, Lesson 1

1. 안녕하세요.
   [an-nyeong-ha-se-yo.]
2. 감사합니다.
   [gam-sa-ham-ni-da.]
3. b. [jon-daen-mal]

4. c. [ban-mal]

5. 존댓말
   [jon-daen-mal]

Answers for Level 1, Lesson 2

1. 네.
   [ne.]
2. 아니요.
   [a-ni-yo.]
3. b

4. 맞아요.
   [ma-ja-yo.]
5. e

Answers for Level 1, Lesson 3

1. 안녕히 계세요.
   [an-nyeong-hi gye-se-yo.]
2. 안녕히 가세요.
   [an-nyeong-hi ga-se-yo.]
3. 안녕히 가세요.
   [an-nyeong-hi ga-se-yo.]
4. well-being, peace, health

Answers for Level 1, Lesson 4

1. 죄송합니다.
   [joe-song-ham-ni-da.]
2. 죄송합니다.
   [joe-song-ham-ni-da.]
3. 저기요.
   [jeo-gi-yo.]
4. c (안녕히 가세요 means "goodbye")

5. d

Answers for Level 1, Lesson 5

1. 학생이에요. = I am a student. / He is a
   [hak-ssaeng-i-e-yo.]
   student. / They are students.

2. 의자예요. = It is a chair.
   [ui-ja-ye-yo.]
3. 이거예요. = It is this one.
   [i-geo-ye-yo.]
4. 집이에요. = It is a house. / I am at home.
   [ji-bi-e-yo.]
5. 진짜예요. = It is real.
   [jin-jja-ye-yo.]
6. 물
   [mul]
7. 뭐
   [mwo]
8. 뭐예요?
   [mwo-ye-yo?]
9. 저예요.
   [jeo-ye-yo.]
10. 학교
   [hak-kkyo]

Answers for Level 1, Lesson 6

1. 이거 뭐예요? = What is this?
   [i-geo mwo-ye-yo?]
2. 이거 책이에요. = This is a book.
   [i-geo chae-gi-e-yo.]
3. 이거 = this one, this thing
   [i-geo]
4. 네. 맞아요. = Yes, that is right.
   [ne. ma-ja-yo.]
   / 이거 = this
   [i-geo]
5. 아니요 = No.
   [a-ni-yo]

Answers for Level 1, Lesson 7

1. 이거 - a   2. 저것 - c

3. 그거 - b   4. 그것 - b

5. 저거 - c   6. 이것 - a

7. 저거 뭐예요? = What is that over there?
   [jeo-geo mwo-ye-yo?]
8. 이 컴퓨터 = this computer
   [i keom-pyu-teo]
9. 뭐 = what
   [mwo]
10. 예요 = to be, 예요 = to be
   [ye-yo]   [ye-yo]

Answers for Level 1, Lesson 8

1. 이거 우유 아니에요. = This is not milk.
   [i-geo u-yu a-ni-e-yo.]

2. 그거 모자 아니에요. = It is not a hat.
   [geu-geo mo-ja a-ni-e-yo.]

3. 그거 사자 아니에요. = It is not a lion.
   [geu-geo sa-ja a-ni-e-yo.]

4. 저 학생 아니에요. = I am not a student.
   [jeo hak-ssaeng a-ni-e-yo.]

5. 제 잘못 아니에요. = It is not my fault.
   [je jal-mot a-ni-e-yo.]

Answers for Level 1, Lesson 9

1. 은 & 는
   [eun] [neun]

2. 이 & 가
   [i]   [ga]

3. c (이 책이 is correct)

4. 이거는 좋아요.
   [i-geo-neun jo-a-yo.]

5. 피자는 비싸요.
   [pi-ja-neun bi-ssa-yo.]

6. 피자가 비싸요.
   [pi-ja-ga bi-ssa-yo.]

7. 오늘 날씨는 좋네요.
   [o-neul nal-ssi-neun jon-ne-yo.]

8. 이거 뭐예요?
   [i-geo mwo-ye-yo?]

9. 뭐가 좋아요?
   [mwo-ga jo-a-yo?]

10. 이거는 뭐예요?
    [i-geo-neun mwo-ye-yo?]

Answers for Level 1, Lesson 10

1. 있어요
   [i-sseo-yo]

2. 시간 있어요
   [si-gan i-sseo-yo]

3. 시간 없어요
   [si-gan eop-sseo-yo]

4. 시간은 없어요
   [si-ga-neun eop-sseo-yo]

5. 친구 있어요?
   [chin-gu i-sseo-yo?]

6. 한국 친구 있어요?
   [han-guk chin-gu i-sseo-yo?]

7. 없어요
   [eop-sseo-yo]

8. 물 없어요
   [mul eop-sseo-yo]

9. 재미
   [jae-mi]

10. 재미없어요
    [jae-mi-eop-sseo-yo]

Answers for Level 1, Lesson 11

1. 커피 있어요?
   [keo-pi i-sseo-yo?]

2. 네, 커피 있어요.
   [ne. keo-pi i-sseo-yo]

3. 아니요, 커피 없어요.
   [an-i-yo. keo-pi eop-sseo-yo.]

4. 커피 없어요?
   [keo-pi eop-sseo-yo?]

5. 우유 주세요.
   [u-yu ju-se-yo.]

Answers for Level 1, Lesson 12

1. 맛
   [mat]

2. a

3. b

4. 잘 먹겠습니다.
   [jal meok-kke-sseum-ni-da.]

5. 잘 먹었습니다.
   [jal meo-geo-sseum-ni-da.]

Answers for Level 1, Lesson 13

1. 뭐 먹고 싶어요?
   [mwo meok-kko si-peo-yo?]

2. 더 주세요.
   [deo ju-se-yo]

3. 영화   b. 보고 싶어요.
   [yeong-hwa]   [bo-go si-peo-yo.]
   ⇒ 영화 보고 싶어요.

4. 여행   c. 가고 싶어요.
   [yeo-haeng]   [ga-go si-peo-yo.]
   ⇒ 여행 가고 싶어요.

5. 피자   a. 먹고 싶어요.
   [pi-ja]   [meok-kko si-peo-yo.]
   ⇒ 피자 먹고 싶어요.

Answers for Level 1, Lesson 14

1. 읽고
[ik-kko]
A: 저거 읽고 싶어요.
[jeo-geo ik-kko si-peo-yo.]

2. 저거
[jeo-geo]
A: 아니요. 저거요.
[a-ni-yo. jeo-geo-yo.]

3. 그거
[geu-geo]
A: 네. 그거요.
[ne. geu-geo-yo.]

4. 뭐
[mwo]
B: 이거 뭐예요?
[i-geo mwo-ye-yo?]

5. 책
[chaek]
A: 그거 책이에요.
[geu-geo chae-gi-e-yo.]

Answers for Level 1, Lesson 15

1.

1 = 일, 2 = 이, 3 = 삼 , 4 = 사, 5 = 오, 6 = 륙 or 육,
  [il]   [i]   [sam]   [sa]   [o]   [ryuk] [yuk]
7 = 칠, 8 = 팔, 9 = 구, 10 = 십
  [chil]   [pal]   [gu]   [sip]

2. 사백칠십육
[sa-baek-chil-sim-nyuk]

3. 이천십년
[i-cheon-sim-nyeon]

4. 사천구백원
[sa-cheon-gu-bae-gwon]

5. 영 or 공
[yeong] [gong]

Answers for Level 1, Lesson 16

1. 아요
[a-yo]

2. 여요
[yeo-yo]

3. 어요
[eo-yo]

4. 먹어요
[meo-geo-yo]

5. 해요
[hae-yo]

Answers for Level 1, Lesson 17

1. 팔아요
[pa-ra-yo]

2. 이상했어요
[i-sang-hae-sseo-yo]

3. 기다렸어요
[gi-da-ryeo-sseo-yo]

4. 써요 (NOT 쓰어요)
[sseo-yo]

5. 멋있었어요
[meo-si-sseo-sseo-yo]

Answers for Level 1, Lesson 18

1. 어디
[eo-di]

2. 에
[e]

3. 에서
[e-seo]

4. 에서
[e-seo]

5. 에
[e]

Answers for Level 1, Lesson 19

1. 언제 했어요?
[eon-je hae-sseo-yo?]

2. 언제 일어나요?
[eon-je i-reo-na-yo?]

3. 언제 왔어요?
[eon-je wa-sseo-yo?]

4. 언제 도착했어요?
[eon-je do-cha-kae-sseo-yo?]

5. 아침에 몇 시에 일어나요?
[a-chi-me myeot si-e i-reo-na-yo?]

Answers for Level 1, Lesson 20

1. 스물
[seu-mul]

2. 열한 살이에요.
[yeo-ran sa-ri-e-yo.]

3. 스무 살이에요.
[seu-mu sa-ri-e-yo.]

4. 스물 네 살이에요.
[seu-mul-ne sa-ri-e-yo.]

5. 스물 다섯 살이에요.
[seu-mul-da-seot sa-ri-e-yo.]

6. 스물 일곱 살이에요.
[seu-mul-il-gop sa-ri-e-yo.]

7. 스물 아홉 살이에요.
[seu-mul a-hop sa-ri-e-yo.]

8. 마흔 살이에요.
[ma-heun sa-ri-e-yo.]

9. 쉰 살이에요.
[swin sa-ri-e-yo.]

10. 쉰두 살이에요.
[swin-du sa-ri-e-yo.]

Answers for Level 1, Lesson 21

1. 안 아파요.
[an a-pa-yo.]

2. 버렸어요.
[beo-ryeo-sseo-yo.]

3. 안 버렸어요.
[an beo-ryeo-sseo-yo.]

4. 안 매워요.
[an mae-wo-yo.]

5. 한국어 공부 안 했어요.
[han-gu-geo gong-bu an hae-sseo-yo.]

Answers for Level 1, Lesson 22

1. to clean = c. 청소하다
[cheong-so-ha-da]

2. to exercise, to work out = d. 운동하다
[un-dong-ha-da]

3. to regret = e. 후회하다
[hu-hoe-ha-da]

4. to remember = b. 기억하다
[gi-eo-ka-da]

5. to make an effort, to try hard = a. 노력하다
[no-ryeo-ka-da]

Answers for Level 1, Lesson 23

1. 누구
[nu-gu]

2. (어제) 누가 (왔어요?)
[nu-ga]

3. (이거) 누구 (예요?)
[nu-gu]

4. (어제) 누구 (만났어요?)
[nu-gu]

5. (그거) 누가 (만들었어요?)
[nu-ga]

Answers for Level 1, Lesson 24

1. why = c. 왜
[wae]

2. what = d. 뭐
[mwo]

3. who = a. 누구
[nu-gu]

4. where = e. 어디
[eo-di]

5. how = b. 어떻게
[eo-tteo-ke]

6. (얼마)였어요?
[eol-ma-yeo-sseo-yo?]

7. (얼마나) 자주 와요?
[eol-ma-na ja-ju wa-yo?]

8. (얼마나) 무거워요?
[eol-ma-na mu-geo-wo-yo?]

9. (얼마)예요?
[eol-ma-ye-yo?]

10. (얼마나) 커요?
[eol-ma-na keo-yo?]

Answers for Level 1, Lesson 25

1. a. From Seoul

2. 지금까지
[ji-geum-kka-ji]

3. 내일까지
[nae-il-kka-ji]

4. 여기부터 저기까지, 여기에서 저기까지
[yeo-gi-bu-teo jeo-gi-kka-ji] [yeo-gi-e-seo jeo-gi-kka-ji]

5. 머리에서 발끝까지
[meo-ri-e-seo bal-kkeut-kka-ji]

6. 아침부터 저녁까지
[a-chim-bu-teo jeo-nyeok-kka-ji]

7. 서울에서 부산까지, 서울부터 부산까지
[seo-u-re-seo bu-san-kka-ji] [seo-ul-bu-teo bu-san-kka-ji]

8. 어제부터 지금까지
[eo-je-bu-teo ji-geum-kka-ji]

9. 언제까지?
[eon-je-kka-ji?]

10. 몇 시부터 몇 시까지?
[myeot si-bu-teo myeot si-kka-ji?]

Wow!

You have completed all the lessons in Level 1.

You are doing an amazing job. Keep going!

We will see you in Level 2.

Notes On Using This Book

Romanization

In each lesson, words and expressions are romanized the first time they appear only. Readers are encouraged not to rely on romanization.

Colored Text

Colored text indicates that there is an accompanying audio file. You can download the MP3 audio files at **https://talktomeinkorean.com/audio**.

Hyphen

Some grammar points have a hyphen attached at the beginning, such as -이/가, -(으)ㄹ 거예요, -(으)려고 하다, and -은/는커녕. This means that the grammar point is dependent, so it needs to be attached to another word such as a noun, a verb, or a particle.

Parentheses

When a grammar point includes parentheses, such as -(으)ㄹ 거예요 or (이)랑, this means that the part in the parentheses can be omitted depending on the word it is attached to.

Slash

When a grammar point has a slash, such as -아/어/여서 or -은/는커녕, this means that only one of the syllables before or after the slash can be used at a time. In other words, -은/는커녕 is used as either -은커녕 or -는커녕, depending on the word it is attached to.

Descriptive Verb

In TTMIK lessons, adjectives in English are referred to as "descriptive verbs" because they can be conjugated as verbs depending on the tense.